How to Achieve
Peace of Mind

How to Order:

Single copies may be ordered from Prima Publishing, P.O. Box 1260BK, Rocklin CA 95677; telephone (916) 632-7400. Quantity discounts are also available. On your letterhead, include information concerning the intended use of the books and the number of books you wish to purchase.

How to Achieve Peace of Mind

Your Guide for Attaining Physical, Mental,
Emotional, and Spiritual Well-Being

Jerry Dorsman
and
Bob Davis

Prima Publishing
P.O. Box 1260BK
Rocklin, CA 95677

Production by Jane Gilligan, Bookman Productions
Copyediting by Antonia Moore
Typography by Bookman Productions
Interior design by Paula Goldstein, Bookman Productions
Cover design by Lindy Dunlavey, The Dunlavey Studio
Cover photograph by Richard Hamilton Smith

Library of Congress Cataloging-in-Publication Data

Dorsman, Jerry.
    How to achieve peace of mind : your guide for attaining physical, mental, emotional, and spiritual well-being / Jerry Dorsman, Bob Davis
        p.   cm.
    Includes bibliographical references and index.
    ISBN 1-55958-485-8
    1. Peace of mind.   2. Self-help techniques.   I. Davis, Bob (Robert Hambling).   II. Title.
BF637.P3D67   1994
158'.1—dc20   94-1606
                                                                            CIP

94 95 96 97 98 RRD 10 9 8 7 6 5 4 3 2 1
Printed in the United States of America

To those who by making themselves more peaceful
will make the world more peaceful

Contents

Your Guide to Inner Peace

Preface

Stressed out?

Don't take a tranquilizer, yell at a friend, or kick your dog. It won't help to sedate yourself or blame your troubles on something outside of you. Instead, look within. Why? Because you have the power to change your life.

How to Achieve Peace of Mind contains more than a hundred ways to help you find this power. With it, you can learn to calm yourself, relax at will, improve your outlook and your relationships with others, and even add years to your life. If you want this power, this book is for you.

In preparation for the book, we have studied and practiced hundreds of methods for attaining inner peace. Here we offer those we believe are the most effective, practical, and easiest to use. We've also applied these methods with great success in stress-management classes, therapy groups, and one-on-one counseling sessions.

By achieving peace of mind, you will live more fully. In terms of satisfaction with life, you will be repaid many times over for each moment you spend cultivating peacefulness. Your family, your friends, and your work will all benefit.

How to Achieve
Peace of Mind

Introduction

*H*ow easy is it for an individual to find happiness in today's world? Before answering this question, consider these facts: Since 1960 the United States has seen a 560 percent increase in violent crime, more than a 400 percent increase in illegitimate births, a quadrupling of the divorce rate, and more than a 200 percent increase in teenage suicide. In the 1940s, the top three problems in American schools were talking in class, chewing gum, and making noise; in the 1990s the top three problems are drug abuse, alcohol abuse, and pregnancy. It has been noted that people in the United States change residences an average of once every three years. Pollution is greater on this planet than it has ever been and is getting worse. We are even plagued by "noise pollution" and electromagnetic fields. Furthermore, each day we are subjected to an endless barrage of negative information from the media. Our cities are overcrowded, and many nations of the world have serious population problems.

Most of us would agree that we live in a rootless, restless world. We cannot help being affected by the jarring environment that surrounds us. Indeed, it infringes on almost everyone's peace of mind.

An ancient Chinese curse says, "May you be born in interesting times." This is considered a curse rather than a blessing because your mind will be drawn outward, away from that which gives lasting satisfaction. Our times are certainly *interesting*, in the

1

sense that there is so much happening each minute, so many changes to contend with, so many lures pulling us out of ourselves. Living in these interesting times, we have a greater need for peace of mind than ever before.

WHAT CAN YOU DO?

Do you know that you already have peace within you? It's there, waiting for you to find it.

Every person who has found peace of mind will tell you this: we cannot be happy in the world unless we first find peace within ourselves. But once we find it, we can enjoy the world and all the good things that it offers.

"There is no joy but calm," said the poet Alfred, Lord Tennyson, equating happiness with inner peace. In today's world, where the pace of living is far more frenzied than in Tennyson's day, his choice bit of wisdom has even greater relevance. To experience joy, we must have a calm mind, unclouded by obsessions, compulsions, and feverish excitement. Our serenity then brings happiness.

To start this process in your personal life, accept the challenge we all face in these times, the challenge of achieving peace of mind. This requires some effort on your part, but the rewards are well worth it.

As you create peace in yourself, you increase peace in the world by adding one more peaceful person to it. In addition, when you see the world through serene eyes, you generate peace wherever you go.

HOW THIS BOOK CAN HELP YOU

Here you will find practical, proven methods for attaining peace of mind. Each method is explained step by step, showing you how to implement it in your life.

Some of these methods have been used successfully for centuries by people of many cultures. Other methods have resulted from recent developments in the fields of psychology, sociology, biochemistry, biotechnology, physics, and even home improvement. You will learn how such practices as mental affirmation, celebrating the body, listening, conscious eating, saying no to the media, saying yes to life, and even "letting yourself go crazy" can deepen your inner peace.

This book presents a whole-person approach. It is divided into four parts—physical, mental, emotional, and spiritual—which represent all four aspects of your personal well-being. Working on all four parts of yourself ensures an integrated approach to peacefulness.

Each of the four parts contains more than twenty-five methods. You'll find that these methods vary in nature from active to passive. For instance, in Part One, you'll discover ways of both moving and relaxing your body to achieve peace. In Parts Two and Three, you'll learn that sometimes it's helpful to pay attention to things, such as your breath or what you are doing this very moment, and sometimes it's helpful to relax the focus of your attention in order to see the world differently or to drop an existing thought.

As part of its overall plan, this book offers a juxtaposition of opposites, but you'll find that these "opposing" methods actually complement one another. By combining them, you'll create a greater balance in your life.

In each of us, there's a place free of anxiety, troubles, cares, and worries. This book offers more than a hundred ways to get there. Choose the ways that work best for you.

HOW TO USE THIS BOOK

First, think of this book as a cookbook with numerous, diverse recipes. It is not necessary to read it from cover to cover. Rather, you may want to select the recipes that look good to you and read them. Trust your intuition in this process; it's your best guide.

Second, we recommend making a list of the methods that most appeal to you. We suggest that you include two methods from each of the four parts to create a whole-person approach. Remember, all the parts work together. For instance, it is difficult to use the mental relaxation methods if you consume a lot of sugar, drugs, or alcohol, because these substances increase nervous tension.

Third, once you've made your selection, go back and read the methods thoroughly. If they still seem right to you, start using them on a regular basis.

Finally, go back and choose three or more additional methods from anywhere in the book. Select methods that you think will work for you and that you have time to incorporate into your life. For instance, Slow-Motion Movement or Awakening the Memory take time to practice, while "shift in perspective" methods, such as the Stop techniques, Gratitude, and Watching the Breath can be done anywhere.

If after working with a method, you find it doesn't feel right for you, discontinue it and select another. Different methods work for different people, and your inner peace is a personal affair. So be true to yourself and practice the methods you enjoy most.

PART ONE

Physical Peace

If anything is sacred, the human body is sacred.
— *Walt Whitman*

*F*or each of us, peace begins at home. And because we live in our bodies, the body is home.

But more than a home, the body is a sanctuary. It is the source of our energy, the abode of our feelings, the seat of our soul. It offers us a sacred place in which to dwell. By treating the body well, we create the foundation for inner peace.

How do we treat the body well? Here are a few essential ways:

- See your body as a thing of beauty, which it is.
- Honor it.
- Respect it.
- Energize it through various activities.
- Give it time for peaceful rest.
- Nurture it with wholesome food.
- Pamper it.
- Show thanks for the joy it brings you.

This section offers practical methods for achieving inner peace through the body. All of these methods will help to reduce physical tension as well as establish optimal health and well-being. Some are active, such as exercise, yoga, and dancing. Some are restful, such as deep breathing and "letting go." And some are nourishing, such as enjoying a peaceful meal.

So this is your entry point. Pick two techniques from this section and build your foundation for inner peace.

CHAPTER 1

Our Bodies in Motion

*H*ow do you feel about your body? If you're like most people, you're a little self-conscious about the way it looks and you don't always treat it as well as you'd like.

But this body is the source of your energy. And, like it or not, it gives back to you only as much as you put into it.

In December 1961, John F. Kennedy, in one of his presidential addresses, said: "We are under-exercised as a nation. We look instead of play. We ride instead of walk. Our existence deprives us of the minimum of physical activity essential for healthy living." Has much changed since Kennedy spoke these words? In November 1993, Lauran Neergaard of the Associated Press reported: "Americans know they need to exercise more for good health. But a new survey [conducted by President Clinton's Council on Physical Fitness and Sports] shows they have no intention of doing it." This survey of 1,018 Americans showed that most of them wanted better health but felt "too tired" or "too lazy" to exercise.

Obviously, these people didn't know the facts about exercise. If they had, they would have realized that they could solve the problems that kept them from exercising simply by exercising. This is because exercise energizes the body, thereby eliminating tired and lazy feelings.

In addition, exercise produces endorphins. These naturally occurring biochemicals act as tranquilizers in the body. They relax and calm us.

Could you ask for any better set of reasons to start exercising and, once you do, to keep it up? Through the methods in this chapter, you will enter your body and joyfully become one with it.

CELEBRATING THE BODY

We ought to dance with rapture that we should be alive, and in the flesh, and part of the living, incarnate cosmos.

—D. H. Lawrence

When we were young, we were sensuous and playful and we naturally celebrated our bodies. Intent on understanding the strangeness and beauty of the world, we used all five senses to open ourselves to life. This is why, when we think back to our childhoods, we remember a time when even the simplest movements we made were magical. Winding up and spinning on swings, skipping to our own inner rhythms, or waving our hands like birds' wings, we celebrated our physical selves.

As Diane Ackerman said in her book, *A Natural History of the Senses*, "We need to return to feeling the textures of life. Much of our experience in twentieth-century America is an effort to get away from those textures, to fade into a stark, simple, solemn, puritanical, all-business routine that doesn't have anything so unseemly as sensuous zest."

To celebrate the body, that miraculous form we assumed at birth, we must reconnect with our senses and live through them, the way we did as children. This will heighten another sense as well: our sense of wonder. After all, what is the sense of wonder— our sixth sense that delights in the other five—if not a special appreciation for life's abounding mysteries?

Science now challenges the notion that the mind exists solely in the head. The most recent discoveries in physiology indicate that the mind journeys through the entire body via enzymes and hormones, carrying the information we receive from our five senses. So in these terms, the mind is sensuous. It creates intimate connections within us.

Try this:

Think of your body as a habitat of enjoyment, a place which, for at least a certain period each day, you will enter and explore. During this time, focus on being an animal, moving like a bird or deer, gracefully alive. Go for a walk in the country, dance in your room, or, if you remember what seemingly absurd act you performed as a child to enchant and delight your senses, do it again and do it playfully. Whatever you choose to do, give yourself over to the feelings of your body as you move through that act. Be as keen as a wild animal. If you touch something, attune yourself to your sense of touch, as if you *were* your hand. Feel the impulses rising through your feet as you walk. Attend to the swing of your arms, the turn of your head, the oxygen pumping through your lungs.

When you finish your playful movement, close your eyes; then slowly and lovingly stroke your arms and your face. Sit quietly in gratitude for the life that pulses through you. As the Sufi poet Rumi said, "The throbbing vein will take you farther than any thinking."

This practice will refresh you and increase your zest. Celebrating your body on a regular basis gives you short, much-needed vacations from your daily routine and expands your peace of mind.

Recommended Reading

A Natural History of the Senses by Diane Ackerman. New York: Vintage Books, 1991.

MOVING TO A BEAT

Every day I count wasted in which there has been no dancing.
—Friedrich Nietzsche

Do you like dancing? Do you enjoy moving your body to a beat? Most of us do, because dancing lifts our spirits.

Dancing creates energy. It excites our life force. It stirs us physically, emotionally, mentally, and spiritually, and integrates all of these elements. That is why, simply by dancing, we can experience joy.

When moving our bodies rhythmically, we feel connected to our inner selves. We feel at one. When moving our bodies through space, we feel connected with the world around us.

Dancing tunes the body. Dancing awakens the spirit from deep within, shakes it loose, and sets it free.

You don't even need to play music. You can dance to the music that you hear within. When you set your body in motion, there's music in the movement. Spin yourself into a whirl right now and feel the music begin: the rhythmic motion of your body charms the music out of you. That's how powerful dance is. It creates music all by itself.

What else does dance do? It dissipates nervous tension. It helps to heal your body from disease. It also produces endorphins that induce relaxation and peace of mind.

∞ ∞

Try this:

Dance. Dance to real music or dance to your own imagined music. Set the rhythm within and let your body move in harmony with itself. Be loose. Let the motion take over and set you free.

For this to happen, you must remain uninhibited. So drop all fears about how you look, release all cares about whether you're doing the right step, and don't worry if you miss a beat. If you're self-conscious, practice dancing alone until you feel comfortable with yourself. If you're in a group, don't worry about what other people are thinking. "The solar system has no anxiety about its reputation," said Ralph Waldo Emerson. When dancing, be like the solar system.

Also, don't bother with alcohol or drugs. Even though drinking and drugging make you feel uninhibited, they block your total participation.

As you enter the dance, become wholly involved. Release all of your energy into the dance: it will put you at peace with yourself.

Recommended Reading

These three catalogs list various dance programs:

Whole Dance Catalog from The Center for the Dances of Universal Peace, P.O. Box 626, Fairfax, CA 94978. Phone: (415) 453-8159.

Kripalu Catalog from Kripalu Center, Box 793, Lenox, MA 01240. Phone: (413) 448-3135.

Omega Catalog from Omega Institute, 260 Lake Drive, Rhinebeck, NY 12572-3212. Phone: (914) 266-4301.

SLOW-MOTION MOVEMENT

If we use our imagination to send vital force to various parts of the body, persistently developing strength, and if we watch our muscles during our exercises or watch them in a mirror, we will soon build up a body so beautiful that even athletes will admire it. The secret of the tremendous effect of slow motion exercise on the muscles and the entire organism lies in the constructive work of the consciousness.

—*Selvarajan Yesudian*

When you move your body slowly, your mind slows to the physical pace and monitors your movements. You become more aware of your body because you are no longer moving it mechanically, but consciously. You cannot raise your arm in slow motion without attending to the movement, without feeling the play of your muscles and the slow upward sweep of your arm.

How does this relate to inner peace? First, by focusing on moving slowly, your mind concentrates. You are no longer distracted, no longer made restless by thoughts. Also, by exercising and stretching, you work the tension from your muscles, the stiffness from your spine. Because of this, slow-motion movement is one of the best ways to achieve inner peace by harmonizing your body and your mind.

Second, by channeling your mental energy to your muscles, you animate and sensitize your body. This healthy practice leaves you feeling more zestful and energized. When you finish ten or fifteen minutes of slow-motion exercise, you have a renewed appreciation for your body and you feel glad to be alive.

You can choose among many systems of slow-motion movement. Many, but not all, originated in the Orient and are based on the movements of animals. The two most popular systems today are tai chi and hatha yoga.

Tai chi.   Considered both a form of exercise and a martial art, basic tai chi comprises 108 movements, and they are all done in a standing posture. The practice of tai chi originated in ancient China and is practiced today in that country's parks as a form of recreation much like Frisbee or golf in American parks. In recent years, tai chi has become quite popular in the United States, and there are many good books available on the subject, as well as classes and teachers in or near urban communities. The movements are done slowly and meditatively in order to "awaken chi," a vital force of consciousness that can keep the body healthy, prolong life, and bring peace of mind. Unlike those who follow hatha yoga, practitioners of tai chi do not consciously control their breathing. Rather, the practice of this corporal art is said to slow down the breath, making it deep and rhythmic. When the breath is relaxed, the mind is likewise calmed.

Hatha yoga.   An ancient form of exercise that originated in India, hatha yoga is composed of movements and postures that are often named after animals (the Fish, Locust, Camel, Cobra, and Peacock are a few examples). The practice of hatha yoga involves stretching into a posture and then holding it in a stationary manner, while breathing deeply. The rhythmic breathing relaxes the muscles stretched by the posture or *asana*, so that when you come out of the posture, there is a deep release of tension from these muscles. Consequently, those who practice hatha yoga have limber bodies and flexible spines. The postures also massage and channel oxygenated blood to vital organs, glands, and nerves, thus strengthening the immune system so it can better resist disease. Hatha yogis claim that the practice accumulates *prana* in the body, a life force similar or equivalent to *chi*. According to the yoga tradition, the most accessible form of *prana* is in the air we breathe. Hence, the practice of deep rhythmic breathing is combined with the stretches and postures.

Other forms of slow-motion movement.   The traditions of dance and, more recently, movement therapy have spawned additional slow-motion exercises. The practice of Zen meditation involves alternating periods of sitting and walking; the walking is done slowly and consciously. In fact, you can do many activities, from cleaning the house to swimming, in slow motion: experiment to learn what best connects your body with your mind and makes you feel healthier and more peaceful.

Try this:

When doing slow-motion exercises, it is important to apply the following principles to your practice.

Before you begin, take a few deep breaths and relax. Center yourself in your body.

Begin moving very slowly, without a sense of rush or a goal in mind. Keep feeling your body as you move, inhabiting it completely. Feel the muscles and nerves involved with each movement. Don't push or strain yourself. These suggestions will help you to become immersed in the practice and feel deeply relaxed afterward.

To master the art of slow-motion movement, practice regularly for short periods of time. Try to practice at the same time each day on an empty stomach. (When you've just eaten, digestion competes for your inner energy.) At first, ten to fifteen minutes of practice will be fine. Don't overdo it. Eventually you can work up to half-hour or hour-long sessions.

Be relaxed and playful while you exercise. Don't do it compulsively. If you undertake the practice with no goal in mind —whether to lose weight, stop smoking, or gain inner peace— you will often find that these healthful results come about naturally, along with other benefits you never considered.

At the end of each session, lie down on your back, close your eyes, and take a few moments to relax your entire body. Imagine yourself absorbing all the life force which your practice has freed up. This will deepen your appreciation for the practice and strengthen your resolve to make it a part of your life.

Recommended Reading

T'ai Chi: the Supreme Ultimate Exercise for Health, Sport and Self-Defense by
    Man-Ching Cheng and Robert W. Smith. Rutland, VT:
    Tuttle, 1965.

The Wandering Taoist by Ming-Dao Deng. New York: Harper and
    Row, 1983.

Yoga and Health by Selvarajan Yesudian and Elisabeth Haich.
    London: Unwin, 1953.

Yoga: The Iyengar Way by Silva, Mira & Shyam Mehta. New York:
    Knopf, 1992.

KNEADING THE BODY

Happiness lies in the fulfillment of the spirit through the body.

—*Cyril Connolly*

Each of us is teeming with energy—electrical energy, mechanical energy, chemical energy. This energy moves within us, keeping us not only alive but also constantly changing.

When our energy flows freely, we feel vital, healthy, and at peace. Unfortunately, our energy often gets blocked in various places throughout the body. This blockage or stagnation is caused by poor diet, poor posture, lack of exercise, too much exercise, injuries, muscle strain, fatigue, or substance abuse.

Massage is an excellent way to release this blocked energy and alleviate bodily pain. A massage soothes the entire body. It reduces tension, and liberates our natural vigor for life. Many body work practitioners claim that massage releases great healing power in the body.

Options:

Exchanging massages with loved ones or friends is always a good idea. But be sure to try a few sessions with one or more local professionals. You'll be amazed at how good a professional can make you feel.

When seeking a professional massage, you may find the following descriptions helpful:

Acupressure/Shiatsu. Based on the acupuncture medical model for improving energy flow in the body, acupressure and shiatsu involve deep pressing with fingers, knuckles, and thumbs. This warming process increases circulation, relieves tension, and helps to heal internal organs.

Chiropractic. By correcting any misalignment of the spine, chiropractic frees nerve pathways between the mind and the body. It can relieve backache and neck ache as well as reduce nervous tension.

Polarity therapy. Based on electrical energy flow in the body, this treatment balances positive and negative currents. Polarity therapy has been proven effective with many types of pain, including emotional pain.

Rolfing.   This is perhaps the most intense and comprehensive of all massages (it takes ten sessions to complete the course). Rolfing involves everything from a soft, soothing touch to a hard, almost painful kneading of deep tissue. It helps to realign the body, balance the mind, correct internal energies, and heal bodily organs.

Sports massage.   More active rubbing with an open hand characterizes sports massage. It involves some percussion or drumming on the body and is good for relieving muscle tension and for increasing circulation.

Swedish massage.   Softer than acupressure, Swedish massage is distinguished by long, smooth strokes, usually with an open hand. This relaxing, warming treatment releases muscular tension and improves energy flow through the body.

NEEDLING THE BODY

When I returned to my family after acquiring acupuncture skills, it appeared as wizardry that a few needles placed strategically could perform instant wonder.

—Harriet Beinfield, L.Ac.

Acupuncture involves the insertion of small needles under the skin in order to activate the energy flow within the body. In China, where the practice originated, this energy is called *chi*, which means "life force."

You can receive acupuncture treatments for almost any kind of ailment, including simple pain. But the treatment that may aid most in achieving peace of mind is the one that's used to treat depression, anxiety, and withdrawal from alcohol. An acupuncturist places five very thin, short needles on outer ear points for thirty to forty-five minutes. This treatment is so basic that it can be done in a waiting room, on a walk-in basis.

How does it work? Stimulation of these points on the outer ear creates an energy exchange with the brain that automatically produces endorphins. Instantly, you experience a natural high—without the use of drugs. Not only is the treatment completely painless, but it generates euphoria. Eighty percent of individuals receiving this treatment report an improvement in how well they feel.

One variation on acupuncture is CES. CES stands for Cranial Electrotherapy Stimulation (also known as NET, which stands for Neuro-Electric Therapy). For CES, adhesive electrodes are attached to ear points—behind the ear, so as to be less visible—and wires connect to a stimulator. The stimulator, worn on a belt or put in a pocket, has a button that can send a mild current to ear points. This current causes stimulation similar to the needles, making the brain produce endorphins. The bonus with CES is this: you can get the stimulation anytime you need it. If you feel a little down, just press a button.

Try this:

Go for an acupuncture (or CES) treatment. Look for acupuncture clinics or holistic health centers in your area. Also check alcohol and drug treatment centers; many now offer acupuncture on an outpatient basis.

You may even want to get your own CES machine. If you're interested in this option, here are two resources:

Tools for Exploration
San Rafael, CA
For catalog, call: 800-456-9887

Inner Quest
Kansas City, MO
For catalog, call: 800-628-MIND

Recommended Reading

For information on acupuncture: *Between Heaven and Earth: A Guide to Chinese Medicine* by Harriet Beinfield, L.Ac., and Efrem Korngold, L.Ac., O.M.D. New York: Ballantine Books, 1991.

For information on CES/NET: *Hooked? NET: The New Approach to Drug Cure* by Meg Patterson, MBE, MBChB, FRCSE. London: Faber & Faber, Ltd., 1986.

TOUCH AND GO TECHNIQUES

The art of life lies in a constant readjustment to our surroundings.
—*Okarkura Kakuzo*

You have already learned about two types of bodywork, massage and acupuncture. This section explores another type of bodywork, which combines massage with specific forms of bodily movement. The "touch and go" techniques, in general, work to retrain your body so that you can move freely. Each can help to reduce stress, improve vital energy, and heal.

∽ ∽

Options:

Alexander Technique.   As you go through normal movements such as walking or sitting, a trainer repositions your body, particularly your spine, to help you achieve greater balance. This teaches you to move effortlessly and results in better posture.

Aston Patterning.   Deep tissue massage combined with movement education and fitness training, help you to break harmful

patterns of movement and to find your own "personal pattern."
Comfort in movement is enhanced.

Feldenkrais Method.   A series of "body lessons" increases your
awareness of inner movement, your flexibility, and your coordi-
nation. Therapists move your body and use light touch to help
you be more relaxed when you're active.

Hellerwork.   Three elements—massage, movement education,
and dialogue—are combined. The dialogue part is psychothera-
peutic, helping you to release difficult memories or feelings of
self-consciousness.

Physical therapy.   Traditionally used to help with physical
injuries, methods of physical therapy alleviate pain and bring
about greater functional movement. Physical therapy also proves
effective in treating numerous neurological problems, such as
stroke, and various diseases, such as heart disease and cancer.

Trager Approach.   To release painful mental and emotional patterns that are trapped in your body, therapists may shake, rock,
or stretch various parts of your body, as well as move each joint
or muscle through its range of motion.

These methods work with varying degrees of effectiveness
for different individuals. Some techniques produce results for
some individuals but not for others. Experiment to discover
which methods work best for you.

You can find listings of practices that employ these techniques by checking any "New Age" directory in your area. Or
look through alternative-press newspapers, alternative medicine
guides, and magazines, often available at health food stores. If
you have a holistic health center nearby, call and ask for information on what they offer.

ₒUTER MOTION TO INNER PEACE

ₒₒ, the wild joys of living! the leaping from rock up to rock,
The strong rending of boughs from the fir-tree, the cool silver shock
Of the plunge in a pool's living water.

—*Robert Browning*

As you probably know, physical activity builds physical strength. With exercise, your muscles improve, your body tone revives, even your internal organs get stronger.

But here's something you may not know: physical activity leads to inner bliss. It's true. Scientists have pinpointed a bio-chemical reason for this. During physical activity, the body produces endorphins. These naturally occurring tranquilizers have a powerfully calming effect and create a natural high.

Without physical exercise, you can become nervous and depressed; your life may seem dreary and dull. Tennyson once said, "I myself must mix with action, lest I wither by despair." This holds true for all of us. Therefore, to achieve greater peace of mind, become as active as you can.

How do you get active? Plan your own exercise program and begin doing it.

∞ ∞

Try this:

Choose some aerobic exercise, some casual exercise, or a combination of the two.

1. *Aerobic exercise.*   This is a highly active, uninterrupted physical workout that lasts at least twenty minutes. This kind of exercise strengthens your heart and circulation, leaving you feeling relaxed for twelve to twenty-four hours.

Aerobic exercise produces an abundance of endorphins. Perhaps you've heard of "runner's high." It describes the point in your workout when you begin to feel euphoric, usually after twenty minutes of vigorous activity.

You will gain the greatest benefits by planning three or four aerobic workouts per week. Scientific studies show that the heart begins to lose the benefits of conditioning when more than two days go by without exercise. So if you exercise on Monday, you will need to exercise again by Wednesday and no later than Thursday in order to keep your heart fit.

Be sure to select exercises that are fun for you and easy to do. Also, keep in mind that you don't have to do the same thing all the time. You have many options. Let's say you already play soccer on Saturdays; then you can plan a brisk walk for Mondays, go jogging on Tuesdays, and work out on the rowing machine in your basement on Thursdays.

As important as exercise is, it's also important not to become obsessed with it. For instance, don't be overly concerned about timing workouts or losing weight on a particular schedule.

One last suggestion: after an aerobic workout, relax. First, you might want to take a few minutes for "cool-down" exercises, such as stretches. Then take ten to fifteen minutes to do nothing, absolutely nothing. During this time, you can appreciate how relaxed you feel.

2. *Casual exercise.*   This is any physical activity not vigorous enough or not long enough to be aerobic. Our lives are filled with casual exercise. Just walking from room to room is a casual exercise.

The worst thing you can do is lie around. You'll only get depressed—and stay that way. It becomes a vicious circle: lying around makes you depressed, and when you're depressed, what's the only thing you want to do? Lie around.

So don't get caught in this trap. Plan to be as active as possible. Instead of using your car, walk or ride your bike. Instead of escalators or elevators, take the stairs. Use your own human power instead of machines. Use a handsaw instead of a power saw, use a push mower instead of a riding mower, wash the dishes by hand instead of using a dishwasher, and so on.

Here are some suggestions:

- Go for walks. Walking is one of the easiest and most beneficial forms of exercise.
- Fully involve yourself in any physical activity that is part of your daily routine.
- Do stretching exercises (such as yoga).
- Try some of the energy-balancing exercise systems (such as tai chi, kung fu, or aikido).
- Play. Play often, play hard, enjoy.

CHAPTER 2

Our Bodies at Rest

*W*hen you take time to relax, do you know how? Most people don't. For instance, when taking a break from work, most people eat something sweet, drink coffee or a soda, or smoke a cigarette.

All of these choices increase your nervous tension. What's worse, caffeine and nicotine increase your heart rate. So if this is how you try to relax, you are defeating your purpose.

In the evening at home, many people think they're relaxing when they watch TV. But the results of a thirteen-year study by psychologists Robert Kubey of Rutgers University and Mihaly Csikszentmihalyi of the University of Chicago proved that television makes viewers moody. The study showed that people are less relaxed after watching TV—even when their reason for watching in the first place was "to relax."

In this chapter, you'll learn a few key ways to relax when your body is at rest. For instance, you'll discover how to improve your peace of mind by becoming attentive to your breath, by using a progressive relaxation method, and by creating a more healthful environment in your home.

THE MUSIC OF THE BREATH

If you would foster a calm spirit, first regulate your breathing; for when that is under control, the heart will be at peace; but when

breathing is spasmodic, then it will be troubled. Therefore, before
attempting anything, first regulate your breathing on which your
temper will be softened, your spirit calmed.

—*Kariba Ekken*

If you notice your breathing when you are anxious or upset, you'll
find that it's quick and irregular and that your diaphragm is tensed.
But if you notice your breathing when you are relaxed, you will see
that it is calm and moves with a slow, steady rhythm, as if to music.
You can orchestrate and enjoy this music by relaxing your stomach
muscles and allowing your diaphragm to move freely, back and
forth, from where it is attached by connective tissue to your lower
ribs. This fills the lower lobes of your lungs and brings your breath
all the way through the upper parts of your lungs and the bronchial
passages. You will aerate your lungs fully, expanding their tiny air
sacs, or alveoli, and maximize the exchange of oxygen and carbon
dioxide. Deep rhythmic breathing will enrich your blood with
oxygen and cleanse your body of impurities and toxins. A ten- or
fifteen-minute session will leave you feeling refreshed, revitalized,
and relaxed.

ᘓ   ᘓ

Try this:

Lie down on your back and draw your feet up, placing them
flat on the floor, hip width apart, with your heels close to your
buttocks. Place one hand on your stomach below your lowest
ribs and the other hand on your chest above your sternum. Let
your elbows rest on the floor, so that you can relax your arms.
Close your mouth, place the tip of your tongue on your upper
palate, behind your front teeth. Shut your eyes, and feel how
you are breathing. Do you feel the movement of your diaphragm
beneath your lower hand, or do you feel your breath primarily in
your chest? Is your breath deep or shallow, rhythmic or erratic?
       Now contract your stomach muscles by exhaling, and
empty your lungs. You can even press down on your stomach
with your hand to get the feel of contracting these muscles and

forcing the air from your lungs. Then breathe in, relaxing your stomach muscles, letting them expand to their capacity. As you do this, think of using your stomach muscles to raise your lower hand as high as possible. Inflate the lower lobes of your lungs and then allow your breath to move up through your lungs; feel your rib cage expand and then your chest rise beneath your upper hand. When this happens, your lower hand will descend as your stomach flattens at the peak of your inhalation.

Now, as you breathe out, contract your abdominal muscles and flatten your stomach (you can press down again with your hand if that helps). Think of curling your stomach muscles up and under your rib cage. This will build muscular control, strengthen your abdominal muscles, tone your waistline, and massage your digestive organs. Keep breathing out and feel your rib cage closing and then the slight falling of your chest under your hand as you empty the upper parts of your lungs and your bronchial passages.

Inhaling and exhaling this way creates deep, rhythmic breathing that uses your entire lung capacity. It is important to begin the practice with an exhalation, to rid your lungs of carbon dioxide, so they can inflate fully. Keep breathing with your eyes closed and with your hands on your stomach and chest, feeling the movement of your anatomy—abdomen, rib cage, chest. (To feel the rib cage, place your hands on your sides, below your chest, and let your upper arms and elbows rest on the floor. In the middle phase of a breath, you will feel your rib cage swelling and contracting as you inhale and exhale.)

It is also a great help to think of a wave rising in the region of your stomach and flowing upward through your body to your neck. Each time you inhale, the crest of a new wave begins in the region of your stomach and rises to your chest. Each time you exhale, the wave smooths out.

Recommended Reading

The Concise Light on Yoga by B.K.S. Iyengar. New York: Schocken
    Books, 1982.

LETTING GO

Lie down and listen to the crabgrass grow,
The faucet leak, and learn to leave them so.

—*Marya Mannes*

From the standpoint of inner peace, tension is nothing but trapped energy—energy held in the body or mind, where it remains untapped. The purpose of conscious relaxation is to release this energy, so that we feel rejuvenated and enjoy greater health and vitality.

So much of our tension is unconscious. Because we are seldom aware of our unused energy, it can be debilitating. Of course, people say "I feel tense" or "my neck is tight," which localizes the tension in a vague way. But when we become distinctly aware of tension, we facilitate its release.

Try this simple experiment. Close your eyes and focus your entire attention on your face. Don't move, don't touch your face; simply notice the way it feels.

You will immediately become conscious of pockets of tension, usually along your jaw, around your mouth, your cheeks, or in all those twitchy little muscles around your eyes. And through this very attentiveness, you can automatically relax many of these tension areas. This is important to understand, before practicing the art of deep relaxation. So let's state it again, in a slightly different way: you can relax simply by becoming conscious of your tension.

When you consciously probe each part of your body during progressive relaxation, you become aware of how much tension you keep within. If you have an excess of tension, you may feel uncomfortable after trying the exercise that follows. If this is the case, be patient and persist: the art of relaxation is well worth the time you spend mastering it, and it soon becomes one of life's greatest pleasures.

Try this:

Lie down on your back on a rug or relatively firm surface. For best results, at least at first, don't do this in your bed, because you may fall asleep. Remember, the object is to relax deeply yet *consciously*.

Tense your entire body. Squeeze your fists and rigidly tighten your legs and arms; next tighten your abdomen and chest, and clamp your teeth; then open your mouth, stick out your tongue, and make an awful face. Now let go of everything. Let your arms and legs flop on the floor, and close your eyes. If you feel particularly tense, do this clenching, squeezing, and tensing a second time, and then let your body go limp once again.

With your eyes closed, shift in any way you need to, making yourself as comfortable as possible. Then stop moving.

Bring your attention to your breath. Without controlling or changing it, notice how you are breathing. If you feel anxious and stressed, you will find that the rhythm of your breath is quick and erratic. Simply note it, without trying to alter its rhythm. (Your "breath awareness" is an invaluable gauge of how relaxed you are. You will return to it in a moment, to see how it works.)

Having observed your breathing for a minute or two, shift your focus to your feet and sense how they feel. Probe deeply with your mind, feeling your toes, soles, arches, heels, the tops of your feet, and all their muscles and nerves. Be sensitive to any tight, aching areas. Wherever you find tension, imagine it dissolving and releasing its energy into your body.

Now move up, through your Achilles tendons, calves, hamstrings, knees, and thighs, one at a time, probing the tissues, muscles, and nerves. Wherever you find a tension block, again imagine it dissolving and releasing its pent-up energy.

Continue on this journey, upward, through your body, feeling the anal sphincter, buttocks, hips, abdomen, and diaphragm. Bring each part of your body before your mind's eye and imagine that part releasing its tension. Probe deeply, thoroughly, imaginatively. Don't rush. Spend time on the muscles of your back and shoulders. Immerse your consciousness in your neck until you feel it slacken, the nape easing slightly toward the floor.

Finally, move up to your head and face. Let the jaw slacken. Let your tongue rest motionless in your mouth. Feel your lips, your cheeks, your entire face, sensing any residual tension and visualizing the surrendering of its bottled-up energy. Be especially attentive to areas around the eyes, as well as the eyes themselves, since we store so much tension here. Let go of all tension in the twitchy muscles around the eyes. Let your upper eyelids rest on the lower ones. Don't open your eyes, but let them be completely still in their sockets, as if you were a child again, lying on the grass and gazing up, through the translucent blue sky.

At this moment, go into your brain and watch the thoughts come and go, passing like clouds in the sky. Don't cling to any thought. Simply watch each one without judgment and be attentive to the still, quiet gap between thoughts.

Having done all this, return to your breath and become aware of its rhythm. Feel the rising and falling of your diaphragm. Chances are, you will find yourself breathing very smoothly, evenly, and with a feather-light grace. If this is the case, then your relaxation has served its purpose.

Practice the art of conscious relaxation whenever you have the time and inclination, especially when feeling overly stressed. Always begin and end with your breath, using the movement of your diaphragm to gauge your progress. By practicing progressive relaxation, you will cultivate the ability to let go and relax at opportune times throughout the day.

Recommended Reading

The Secret Path by Paul Brunton. New York: E. P. Dutton, 1935.

CREATING A PEACEFUL ENVIRONMENT

As we begin the 1990s, it is obvious that our great industrial age has taken its toll on Americans. We are now exposed to more toxins and dangers at home than anywhere else. The typical American home is in sad shape, indeed. How healthy is your home?

—Linda Mason Hunter

The very home in which we live can threaten our health and well-being as well as our peace of mind. We're exposed to so many toxins in the home that to get rid of just half of them (or at least some of the more serious ones) can bring dramatic changes.

Common toxins in the home can cause headache, fatigue, depression, nervous tension, and even life-threatening health problems, such as cancer or lead poisoning. It follows that by cleaning up your personal environment, you will become healthier and feel less stressed.

Some guidelines:

1. *Water.* Many sources of drinking water in the United States are unsafe. Since 1974, tests have found more than 2,000 toxic chemicals present in our water. Nearly 200 of these chemicals have been shown to cause cancer or nervous system disorders, while more than 1,600 of them have never been tested for health risks. Various toxins have been found in public water, well water, and bottled water. Hence you should get your water tested. Contact a reputable testing company, and when you receive its findings, ask for recommendations on how to get rid of any contaminants in your water.

2. *Cleaning supplies.* Household cleaners are often high in toxic chemicals. Here's what to avoid: ammonia and ammonia products; oven, drain, and toilet cleaners containing lye; carpet shampoo; bleach; non-biodegradable dish soaps and laundry

detergents; floor wax; furniture polish, shoe polish, silver polish, and copper cleaner. For a list of safe alternative cleaning supplies, get a copy of *The Healthy Home* by Linda Mason Hunter (Emmaus, PA: Rodale Press, 1989). You can also find nontoxic household cleaners at your local natural food store or co-op.

3. *Dry cleaning.* Solvents used in dry cleaning are extremely toxic. Avoid dry cleaning as much as possible. One alternative is to rinse clothes in cold water and have them professionally pressed. If you have clothes dry-cleaned, remove the plastic bags and hang the clothes outside for two to three days; most of the solvent will evaporate.

4. *Aerosol sprays.* One of the most toxic items in the home, these sprays are loaded with cancer-causing hydrocarbons. Don't use hair sprays, antiperspirants, room deodorizers, shoe polish sprays, or spray paints.

5. *Air fresheners.* Whether aerosol or solid, they contain a proven carcinogen, paradichlorobenzene. Avoid air fresheners; they're really air polluters.

6. *Paint, paint thinners, and paint removers.* The solvents in these, plus the mercury in some paints, make them extremely dangerous. Avoid them as much as possible. Paint only in well-ventilated areas and wear a respirator. Wait a week before spending time in a freshly painted room.

7. *Indoor insecticides.* This class of chemicals is strong enough to disrupt or kill living cells, including those in your own body. Avoid professional exterminators (if you can't, make sure they don't use chlordane). Avoid insect repellents with diethyl toluamide (DEET). Do not use insecticide sprays. Do not use yellow hanging strips as they emit toxic chemicals into the air for weeks. For information on safe alternatives, contact the National Coalition Against the Misuse of Pesticides, 701 "E" Street SE, Washington, DC 20003 (Phone: 202-543-5450).

8. *Smoking.* Don't smoke in the house. Carbon monoxide and other toxic fumes will build up, particularly during times of the year when all the windows are kept shut.

9. *Electromagnetic fields (EMFs).*   EMFs are created whenever electricity runs through a wire or an appliance that is switched on. Studies have shown that children living near power lines had four times the leukemia rate of other children and adults had cancers at 1.5 to three times the rate of other adults. High doses of EMFs have also been implicated as causing miscarriages, high blood pressure, and emotional problems such as depression. Experts set a safe limit for exposure to EMFs at 2 milligauss. Neighborhood power lines (when you stand right under them) vary widely in their emissions from 0.5 to 30 milligauss, but the typical number is between 5 and 10. High-tension lines, also known as transmission lines, emit from 20 to 600 milligauss, with an average of 100.

When you touch an operating appliance, your typical milligauss exposure is: electric blanket, 20; television, 100; power drill, 500; blow-dryer, 1,400; electric shaver, 1,600; can opener, 4,000.

Other appliances that produce high EMFs: electric oven and range, 10–300; refrigerator, 5–100; microwave ovens, 5–100; dishwashers and clothes washers, 2–5; clothes dryers, 5–110; coffee makers, 6–29; toasters, 10–60; irons, 12–45; mixers, 58–1400; blenders, 50–220; vacuums, 230–1300; and computers, 5–100. At a distance of more than three feet, EMFs of running appliances drop off considerably (to about 1/100th of the above numbers). How should you deal with daily exposure? Step back from running appliances. Stop using electric can openers, shavers, and blankets. When watching TV, sit far from the set; cut down your viewing time to no more than an hour or two a day. Finally, you may want to obtain a gauss meter to test the EMFs at various locations within your home. That way, you'll know which areas to avoid.

10. *Lawn and garden.*   Keep a chemical-free lawn and garden. Avoid herbicides, pesticides, and weed killers. Don't use a professional lawn-care company unless it specializes in organic products.

11. *Particleboard, fiberboard, and plywood.*   Pressed wood products emit formaldehyde into the air for years. In fact, pressed wood is the major source of formaldehyde contamination in

homes, creating more even than urea-formaldehyde foam insula-
tion. Formaldehyde causes eye irritation, respiratory problems,
nausea, rashes, dizziness, insomnia, depression, and fatigue.
Long-term exposure increases your risk of cancer. In new home
construction, pay more to have solid wood used throughout.
When buying a used home, make sure that pressed wood hasn't
been used in the construction or that the house is at least twelve
years old. Avoid mobile homes unless they're more than fifteen
years old. Avoid shelving, cabinets, and other furniture made
with pressed wood. When remodeling, make sure the contractor
doesn't used pressed wood.

12. *Fabric.* The fabric in furniture, rugs, draperies, and
bedding may release as many as twenty-five to thirty different
chemicals into the air. These have been shown to cause various
physical and nervous system disorders. The basic rule, then, is
to avoid furniture, rugs, draperies, and bedding that have been
treated with chemicals. Don't purchase bedding and furniture
padding made of synthetic fiber or cellulose; the same goes for
polyester fill and foam rubber in pillows. For your fabrics, select
untreated natural fibers such as cotton, linen, or wool. A cotton
futon with cotton batting is the best choice for a bed. Use 100
percent cotton, flannel, linen, or silk sheets; they will not irritate
your skin. Use cotton or wool blankets. Your best choice for
carpeting is wool or cotton rugs that have not been chemically
treated. Avoid "miracle fiber" carpets. Check your floor covering
for a green sticker that says "CRI" on it. CRI stands for Carpet
and Rug Institute, which sets chemical emission standards for
carpets. (If you want information on any specific rug or carpet,
call CRI at 800-882-8846.) Also be aware of the padding you
put under your carpet. Choose jute instead of rubber.

13. *Combustion fumes.* The most deadly combustion fume
is carbon monoxide. Faulty gas appliances alone account for 300
carbon monoxide deaths per year. Make sure your gas furnace
and appliances are operating efficiently and that vents are not
blocked. Do the same for your oil burner. If you ever smell oil or
gas or combustion fumes near your furnace, turn it off and get it

fixed. Make sure that your wood-burning stove or fireplace oper-
ates efficiently and does not draft back into the house. Avoid coal
stoves and kerosene heaters.

14. *Radon.*   This radioactive gas leaks into houses from
the ground, so its concentration is strongest in basements and
crawl spaces and weakest in upper stories. According to the
Environmental Protection Agency (EPA), radon causes 5,000
to 20,000 cases of lung cancer each year, making it second only
to cigarette smoking. Get your home tested for radon. If its
presence is above safe levels, get expert help to fix the problem.

15. *Asbestos.*   This man-made fiber was used extensively in
building materials from 1900 to the 1970s. Unless it's completely
encased, asbestos releases microscopic fibers through normal
decay. When inhaled, these tiny fibers pierce the lung lining and
do not dissolve. They remain in the lungs, causing various
diseases including cancer. You should have a professional inspect
your house and remove any asbestos.

16. *Lead.*   Cases of lead poisoning have been well docu-
mented. Exposure to lead can cause brain damage, blood and
kidney diseases, and even death. Areas of most concern are lead
paint and lead plumbing. As lead paint peels, chips, or flakes, tiny
particles become airborne; they can then be inhaled and cause a
toxic reaction. But removal is tricky because sanding or scraping
sends particles into the air, where they remain for days. That's
why it's sometimes better to paint over lead paint with a non-
lead-based product. With plumbing, the lead from pipes or lead
solder slowly leaches into your water supply. Have your water
checked for lead contaminants, and if you have a problem, pay a
plumber to correct it. Have him install copper or brass, *not* PVC
(polyvinyl chloride), pipes, and use solder which is free of both
lead and antimony.

17. *Aluminum.*   The body has trouble eliminating this
metal. It collects in the tissue and may cause long-term problems,
including nervous system disorders. For instance, aluminum has
been linked to Alzheimer's disease. Research shows that the brain

tissue of people who died of Alzheimer's has, on average, four times the normal amount of aluminum. So the first step is to get rid of your aluminum cookware, as some of the metal leaches into the food. Replace it with cast iron, stainless steel, earthenware, or Pyrex. (Avoid non-stick cookware as the surface material also dissolves into food.) Don't consume food or beverages that have been stored in aluminum cans or aluminum foil. Most antiperspirants have aluminum compounds; don't use them. Avoid antacids with aluminum compounds. Avoid baking powder and baked goods with aluminum compounds (most commercially sold baking powder and baked goods do contain them). Finally, avoid commercial salts with added aluminum compounds; buy a high-grade sea salt or kosher salt instead.

18. *Plastic and styrofoam.* Vinyl chloride, a key component in plastic products, causes cancer in living tissue. This compound has been found to leach into foods and beverages stored in plastic containers. Avoid foods that are sold in plastic containers. Don't store food in plastic containers or plastic wrap. Try not to use plastic and Styrofoam cups or plastic plates and utensils.

19. *Lighting.* Your light bulbs can strain your emotional health. In particular, partial-spectrum lighting has been linked to emotional problems such as depression, and partial-spectrum fluorescent lighting can cause headaches, dizziness, fatigue, and nervous tension. The solution is to install full-spectrum lighting in your home. When choosing full-spectrum fluorescent bulbs, select the newer models from which the low-pitched buzzing noise has been eliminated. To find these specialty lights, try a lighting center or a health food store. For a mail-order catalog, call Verilux (800-786-6850) or Simmons Company (800-533-6779).

20. *On your body.* For clarity of mind and general good health, use the safest products on your skin. Wear natural fiber clothing (100 percent cotton, linen, or silk). Use pure soaps as well as natural-ingredient cosmetics, perfumes, and hair-care products. Remember: if you put it on your body, the product becomes intimate. Make sure that it promotes well-being.

Recommended Reading

The Healthy Home by Linda Mason Hunter. Emmaus, PA: Rodale
Press, 1989.

CHAPTER 3

Nourishing Our Bodies

D o you eat right? When you nurture your body with wholesome food, your body will nurture you with a wholesome life.

In "Savoy Truffle," the Beatles sang: "You know that what you
eat you are, / But what is sweet now, turns so sour." During the past
forty years, dozens of studies have backed this song up by linking
the excessive consumption of sweets to nervous tension, fatigue,
and emotional depression. Numerous other studies have demon-
strated that other foods and substances we consume cause similar,
and sometimes worse, emotional problems. Meanwhile, on the
positive side, dozens of studies have shown that certain foods can
actually make you feel more peaceful and relaxed.

In this chapter, you'll learn which foods to avoid and which
foods to eat more often to promote well-being and a calm state of
mind. You'll also learn how to feel more relaxed during mealtimes
and some ways to show thanks for your food that will leave you in
a peaceful mood.

Enjoy.

EATING CONSCIOUSLY

Food is the most intimate consumer product.

—*Ralph Nader*

In America, not only do we eat fast food, we tend to eat food fast. Many of us rush through meals, not taking the time to appreciate our food.

Also, most of us aren't conscious of eating. We remain distracted when we eat We divert ourselves by talking, reading, watching TV, doing crossword puzzles, listening to music, writing, or simply thinking about something other than the food on our plates.

We rarely give a meal our undivided attention. Yet when we start to pay attention, many things happen. We become aware of the intimate connection we have with our food.

Consider for a moment your connection with food. Eating food is probably the most intimate thing you can do. When you eat, you put something inside of you. You take it in completely. First you crush your food and soften it, then your body extracts essential nourishment, which your blood delivers to all your living cells. It is as if your body becomes one with what you eat. Your body takes what it needs from your food, absorbs it, and discharges the rest.

Sex is similar. You become intimate, in this case, with another person. Physically, you want to absorb that person into yourself, take that person completely inside of you. During sex, you imagine this, and in the intensity of the moment it feels true. With food you don't usually imagine this, but in fact it is true.

The idea is captured in a poem by Walter de la Mare: "It's a very odd thing, as odd as it can be, / That whatever Miss T eats, turns into Miss T."

Conscious eating offers the following benefits:

- better digestion
- better feedback from the stomach (It tells you when it's full, so you won't overeat.)
- better sense of a food's value (When taste and smell make you fully aware of your food, you tend to select foods with higher nutritional value.)

- better health (because of the above three items)
- enhanced enjoyment of food
- greater peace of mind (Through conscious eating, you will feel more at one with the world, more connected, more attuned to nature.)

෨ ෨

Try this:

1. Become fully conscious when eating. Ponder the deep, intimate connection you have with your food.

2. Do nothing else. There's a Zen saying: "While eating, eat; while sleeping, sleep." It means, whatever you're doing, do it totally. When eating, give your attention entirely to your food.

3. Savor the flavor. Be aware of two senses: taste and smell. Through these senses, you appreciate your food.

4. Close your eyes. The sense of sight is strong; the sense of taste and smell are subtle. Looking around can be distracting. With closed eyes, you'll find you can "see" your food more clearly.

5. Chew thoroughly. Break up your food completely. To improve health, Gandhi recommended: "Chew your drinks, and drink your foods."

6. Chew on both sides of your mouth. This produces more saliva, which improves digestion. Moreover, it makes use of all the facial muscles related to chewing, in effect massaging the face. This keeps the face trim and actually reduces the possibility of headaches.

7. Sense the food itself. Feel it inside of you. Enjoy swallowing and the warm feeling food imparts to your stomach. Children often say of food, "It feels so good in my tummy." As an adult, you don't have to lose this feeling. Simply start to pay attention, and you will enjoy your meals as much as you did when you were a child.

FOODS THAT PROMOTE PEACE OF MIND

One cannot think well, love well, sleep well, if one has not dined well.
—Virginia Woolf

Pick up almost any magazine or newspaper today and you will find something written about the benefits of a healthy diet. The reason is simple: the right foods can promote physical health. This has become an established fact. But did you know that the right foods can also promote emotional health? It's true. The foods we choose to eat have a great impact on our emotions.

There are three main categories of food when we consider an item's emotional effect on us. They are: foods that agitate us, foods that weigh us down, and foods that promote peacefulness.

Category One:
Foods That Agitate Us

These foods have an adverse effect on the nervous system. They increase tension. Most of them will calm you momentarily—when you're "high" on them—but as soon as you begin to withdraw, nervousness increases. Prolonged use will drain your energy and cause you to feel worn out or fatigued all the time. (Note: these foods are addictive and usually difficult to give up.)

Sugar.   It calms you for 15 minutes to an hour and then increases your nervous tension, triggering cravings for another dose. Research shows that 60 to 80 percent of Americans have problems controlling their sugar intake. There are many varieties of sugar; refined white sugar, or sucrose, is just one. Others include lactose, fructose, maltose, dextrose, corn syrup, honey, maple syrup, and sorbitol. Various sugars have been added to many foods, so read labels carefully.

Alcohol. Its drug effect wears heavily on the nervous system. Also, alcohol converts to sugar in the body, causing the sugar effect described above. (And because alcohol converts to sugar, it has calories and is therefore considered a "food.")

Drugs. These are nonfoods, but they affect biochemical balances in the body as if they were food. All the illegal drugs (including marijuana) cause shifts in brain chemistry that seriously affect the nerve cells in the body. These drugs should be avoided completely. Also, over-the-counter drugs (including aspirin) contain powerful chemicals that change your internal biochemistry. These should be used sparingly.

Nicotine. This nonfood, usually brought into the body through tobacco smoking, causes brief relaxation followed by agitation. Nicotine increases heart rate; one cigarette, for instance, raises your heart rate for twenty minutes after smoking.

Caffeine. This amphetamine, or "speed" drug, revs up the nervous system directly. It can cause you to feel tense initially, then sluggish as its effects wear off. Though not a food, it's found in many food products—coffee, tea, and chocolate, for instance. It is also added, in its pure chemical form, to many soft drinks.

Category Two:
Foods That Weigh Us Down

Foods in this category sap your energy. They can dull your senses and make you feel tired for hours after a meal. These foods take extra energy to digest or cause specific problems with digestion.

Meats. When you eat meat, cholesterol gets in your bloodstream and slows the blood flow in your body. In addition, meats take a long time to digest. In fact, red meat takes longer to digest than any other food except hard-boiled eggs. Chicken is easier to digest, fish even more so.

Eggs. Very high in cholesterol, they are slow to digest.

Dairy foods. This group includes milk and milk products, such as cheese, butter, yogurt, and sour cream. Dairy foods are very high in cholesterol but easier to digest than meat or eggs. Lowfat alternatives (skim milk, 1 percent milk, etc.) are lower in fat but harder to digest than their whole milk counterparts; that's because the butterfat in whole milk aids its digestion.

Refined grains. White rice, white flour, and white flour products (such as pasta and pastries) are in this group. Compared to their whole grain counterparts, these foods lack nutrients. In fact, it takes more nutrients to digest refined grains than they possess. What happens? The body gives up nutrients in order to digest the refined grains, leaving the body with a net loss of certain vitamins and minerals. Also, because the bran has been removed, these foods act like paste in the intestines. (When reading labels, look for "whole wheat" or "100 percent whole wheat." If you see "wheat flour," read "white flour.")

Oils. Another refined food, oils are pressed most commonly from seeds, grains, or nuts. Oils are fats that slow digestion. Too much oil in your diet will make you sluggish. The best oils are cold-pressed and unrefined. The most intelligent choices are sesame (dark or light), olive, safflower, or canola, which are all low in saturated fats. Avoid oils that have been hydrogenated, such as margarines, and oils that are high in saturated fat. (When cooking, small amounts will do. Use an oil brush to lightly coat the bottom of the pan rather than pouring oil directly into it. Also, purchase a steamer so you can steam your food more often.)

Chemical additives, preservatives, and substitute sugars. These are not foods but have been added to many foods. Watch out! The body treats them as toxins, as foreign to the system. The liver and kidneys overwork to remove them from the body, and long-term intake of these chemicals may have a seriously damaging effect on your cells. Many researchers consider this risk so great that they recommend avoiding all varieties of chemical additives, preservatives, and substitute sugars.

Category Three:
Foods That Promote Peacefulness

If you avoid all of the above, what will you eat? Whole grains, beans, vegetables, seeds, nuts, and fruits. Sound familiar? In study after study, this diet has proven to be the best for maintaining optimal physical and mental health.

The foods in this diet are easy on digestion, impart sound nutrition, and offer steady, evenly burning energy for hours after each meal. In short, these foods will help you to feel good inside, emotionally and physically.

∽ ∽

Try this:

Start yourself on the diet that promotes peacefulness. Try it for two weeks. You'll begin to realize the effects after five days (the usual amount of time it takes for your system to get rid of trapped substances and toxins left from your previous diet). Then, after two weeks, make a decision to continue this diet. You have three main options:

1. *Option One.* Make a decision to avoid foods from the first two categories, and stick to this decision. See how you feel after two weeks.
2. *Option Two.* Make a decision to avoid foods from the first two categories except occasional fish, chicken, or dairy foods. This may be easier if the first option seems too radical or too difficult to maintain. (*Occasional* means three or four servings per week.)
3. *Option Three.* For those who have more than one serious addiction in the first category of foods, make a decision to quit eating the foods in category two and to end one of your

addictions from category one. After two months, quit your second serious addiction from the first category. Wait two more months to quit your third addiction, and so on. Get any special help you need to quit these addictions. (Note that when you quit consuming the foods in category two, it will become easier to break the addictions you have to foods in category one.)

Give one of these options a try, and watch yourself begin to change. Notice, as you change, how much more relaxed you feel.

Recommended Reading

Food and Healing by Annemarie Colbin. New York: Ballantine Books, 1986.
Nourishing Wisdom by Marc David. New York: Bell Tower, 1991.
Sugar Blues by William Dufty. New York: Warner Books, 1975.

HERBAL PEACE

> *A moderate amount of aromatic herbs and spices can be quite healthful: They can aid in digestion, prevent flatulence, help in fat breakdown, tonify, stimulate, relax, and generally please our soul with their aromas.*
>
> —*Annemarie Colbin*

For thousands of years, the scents and fragrances of herbs have been used to affect people's moods. Consider the mood created by burning incense at a spiritual service or the power of various perfumes and body lotions to stimulate sexual desire. A fragrant potpourri may subtly lift your mood, while the scents of certain bath oils relax you. The study and use of aromas to change your mood is now called aromatherapy.

In addition, you can take various herbal remedies internally to reduce stress. They are usually taken in the form of tea.

෨ ෨

Try this:

1. *Aromatherapy.*   This form of herbal healing employs various plants and herbs that impart active ingredients into their scents or aromas. Simply smell or inhale the active ingredients, and you can experience a physical change inside.

Here are a few aromas that are recommended to alleviate depression and nervousness:

almond oil:	relaxant
chamomile:	mood lifter and relaxant
lavender:	relaxant
lemon oil:	mood lifter
melissa:	relaxant
narcissus:	relaxant
peppermint:	mood lifter
pine oil:	mood lifter
rose:	mood lifter
sandalwood:	relaxant
spearmint:	mood lifter
ylang-ylang:	relaxant

For best results, use the pure essential oils of these natural products. The oils can be smelled from the bottle, misted into the air, added to a hot bath, or gently massaged into your skin.

2. *Herbal remedies.*   Usually sipped in tea, the following herbs can reduce stress or change your mood:

chamomile:	relaxant—reduces anxiety, induces sleep
lady's slipper:	reduces anxiety, lifts mood, helps cure depression
passionflower:	sedative—induces sleep
St. John's wort:	reduces anxiety, tension, and fatigue
scullcap:	relieves depression, revitalizes nervous system

valerian: sedative—reduces tension
vervain: sedative—relieves depression and sadness
wood betony: relaxant and sedative—eases nervousness and
                  relieves headaches

Recommended Reading

The Art of Aromatherapy by Robert B. Tisserand. Rochester, VT:
     Healing Arts Press, 1977.
The Herb Book by John Lust, N.D., D.B.M. New York: Bantam,
     1974.
Aromatherapy Workbook by Marcel Lavabre. Rochester, VT:
     Healing Arts Press, 1990.
The Way of Herbs by Michael Tierra, C.A., N.D. New York:
     Washington Square Press, 1980.

THANKFULNESS FOR YOUR FOOD

> *The body is sacred and therefore the nutrition of the body is sacred.*
> —*Marc David*

Perhaps more important than what you eat is how you feel about
what you eat. If you feel nourished by your food, and if you feel
thankful for your food, then the experience of eating will affect you
pleasantly.

Take a moment to consider the value of food. Clearly, food
is the source of life. At a very deep level, your body gives thanks
for the food it receives, because your body receives the nourishment.

Food creates life in you. It feeds every living cell in you, so
that these cells may continue to live. With food, something dies
that you may live. Yet how often do you show your appreciation
for these living things that die? When you think about it, food
bestows a blessing upon you. It blesses you with life.

We often talk about blessing the food before a meal, but the food is a blessing itself. Simply by realizing this, you can begin to fully appreciate your food. Indeed, giving thanks for food is giving thanks for life itself.

∞ ∞

Try this:

1. Before you eat, take a moment to think about each kind of food in the meal and to appreciate it.

2. While eating, enjoy the taste of your food and let this remind you of the nourishment the food gives you.

3. Take a moment before or during a meal to appreciate the source of the food. Imagine the animal or the plant from which your food came, and consider the life force it gave up —the same life force you now receive.

4. Extend a simple, silent thanks to all the people who helped to bring this food to you. Consider those who helped the food to grow, those who carried it to you, and those who had a hand in preparing it for your table.

5. Finally, offer thanks, silently or aloud, for all those with whom the meal is shared, that you may enjoy their company and that they too may participate in this bounty.

PART TWO

Mental Peace

The mind is a strange machine which can combine the materials offered to it in the most astonishing ways.
                                        - -Bertrand Russell

*H*ow marvelous is the mind! It allows us to consider hundreds of possibilities each day and select those we like most. Our minds make connections that can be sources of intense pleasure. In our minds, we can soar to new heights.

On the other hand, our minds can cause problems. Our minds constantly produce thoughts and often these thoughts induce tension or sadness. Sometimes the ceaseless activity of the mind itself can be so distracting that we miss many of life's daily joys.

In this section, you'll discover numerous ways to achieve a positive relationship with your thoughts. This section's overall concept is captured in some verses from the singer Donovan: "First there is a mountain / Then there is no mountain / Then there is."

These lines are based on an idea, attributed to Zen, about how the mind perceives the world. The mind of everyday experience sees the mountain. This mind sees the world as it is and takes it at face value. But the mind of someone who is searching for deeper meaning penetrates reality and finds that things are not always as they appear. Then there is no mountain; it blinks out of sight. Finally, after a period of searching and reorganizing its perspective, the mind discovers the world anew. This is the mind of bliss. To this mind, the mountain reappears—but now the mountain is iridescent, vibrant , and more beautiful than ever before.

You'll experience a similar progression of mental awareness as you work through part two. Let's say you currently perceive reality at the everyday level, perhaps even feeling that your usual perception is somewhat superficial and dull. The methods in chapter 4 will help you free yourself from traditional ways of thinking and see the world in a slightly different way. In chapter 5, you'll reconnect with the world as you generate peacefulness by involving yourself in thought. In chapter 6, you'll learn techniques concerning your two most powerful senses: sight and hearing. With most of these techniques, the world outside of you will disappear, then reappear within. Lastly, in chapter 7, you'll take a look at how the mind perceives time and how to break through this mental conditioning. You will discover how to make time disappear and enjoy the eternal present.

Many of the techniques in these chapters are traditional meditation techniques. Some can be done in an instant, simply by shifting your perspective; others take some time. But before committing *your* time to them, consider this: Gandhi was said to have taken one hour every day for meditation, except when he was really busy. Then he would take two.

CHAPTER 4

Freeing Yourself from Thought

*E*ach day the world is new, different from what it was the day before. To examine the newness with an open mind refreshes us.

The trouble is, most of us miss what's new and different with each new day because the mind insists on finding similarities. The mind seeks things that are the same as those it knew the day before. The mind wants to categorize. It demands continuity so that it can understand things.

In this chapter, you'll discover ways to break many of your mental patterns. These practices will help you to see the world from a new perspective.

YOU ARE NOT WHAT YOU THINK

Sitting quietly, doing nothing, spring comes and the grass grows by itself.

—*Zen saying*

The nature of a human mind is like a TV that's constantly on, flooding each person with images, voices, slogans, memories, fears, highs, lows—an unstoppable barrage. In such a state of ceaseless flux, where is the "I" that's doing the thinking?

If you watch your mind for a while, you'll see that only occasionally do you really "think"—that is, use your mind as a tool to
accomplish a particular endeavor. Most of the time the mind works
like that TV we can never shut off (unless we are in deep sleep). It
entertains, bores, or haunts us with uncontrollable thoughts, willy-
nilly. This realization, though unflattering at first, can help you
greatly with the method that follows.

It's important to understand that much of what we do in life
is based on our identification with particular thoughts that pass
through our minds: we act on these thoughts as if we *were* them.
The results can be good when the thought with which we identify
is positive and life-affirming. At other times, however, this identifying behavior can cause difficulty; lifelong problems can even
result from our momentary actions. For instance, a person who
identifies with a transitory emotional state can commit a crime
which he or she in turn regrets forever after. This happens when
people see themselves as their thoughts: a passing emotion can
color the mind.

∞　∞

Try this:

Sit comfortably in a quiet place. Close your eyes and take a few
deep breaths. Let your body be still. Now begin to watch the
thoughts and images that pass through your mind as though you
were watching a TV show. Consider the mind to be a show
which you are not producing, directing, projecting, or starring
in. Rather, you are sitting in the audience, impassive, indifferent,
simply watching, neither attaching yourself to any one thought
nor identifying with any of them. You are not judging, condemning, inviting, or suppressing thoughts. An impartial attitude is
important to the success of this method.

There will be times when you get caught up in your
thoughts, when you lose yourself in the TV show. The mind is
so seductive that this is inevitable. As soon as you realize you've
been swept up, gently remind yourself to become the impersonal
observer again.

Don't be disheartened by the chaotic, plotless, senseless nature of the interior show. This is how the mind works; you are seeing its ungovernable productions. Simply let the thoughts come and go, interfering with them as little as possible.

What can you gain through this method? First, you will understand the reality of the mind. Through close observation, you will see how it seduces and tyrannizes you. By detaching yourself from your thoughts, you will become more objective and less bothered by what passes through your mind each day. You will develop the ability to see that each mental state, no matter how overwhelming or permanent it seems, will pass in time.

Second, if you practice regularly, you will soon experience a gap between one thought and the next—a cessation of thinking when the TV screen goes blank for an instant. This will happen if you don't try to suppress the flow of thoughts but instead keep witnessing the process without exercising your will on it. In fact, only by watching the mind in this way will you discern the gap between one thought and another. Remember, you cannot stop your thinking. But if you let the mind be, your thinking will stop by itself. By letting all images, thoughts, and sensations arise and then pass without being bothered by them—without reacting, without judging, without clinging, without identifying with them —you will experience inner peace. As your thoughts slow down, your mind quiets by itself.

Finally, this practice will help you to think. By learning not to identify with your thoughts, you will discover how to use the mind when it is meant to be used, to accomplish what you need to do. Your mind will be more of a tool than a tyrant—a tool you can work with when you need it and let go of when you don't need it.

Recommended Reading

Journey of Awakening: A Meditator's Guidebook by Ram Dass. New York: Bantam Books, 1978.

Zen Mind, Beginner's Mind by Shunryu Suzuki. New York: Weatherhill, 1970.

WATCHING THE BREATH

> *Each time we find ourselves dispersed and find it difficult to gain*
> *control of ourselves by different means, the method of watching the*
> *breath should always be used.*
>
> —*Thich Nhat Hanh*

The practice of observing the breath helps create both physical
and mental calm. How? When you take time to watch yourself
breathe, your diaphragm relaxes and your breath becomes regular
and rhythmic. It begins to flow in a wavelike manner. As the breath
becomes restful, the mind becomes restful.

An age-old technique, the practice of breath-watching arose
in diverse civilizations that cultivated inner peace. Many practitioners of this technique have claimed that thinking stops during
the moments between the in-breath and out-breath, and the out-
breath and in-breath. When you achieve this cessation of thinking,
you are free from the mind's tyranny.

℃ ℃

Try this:

1. *Use your imagination.*   Imagine that you are a feather-light
weight lying on top of your abdomen. You are taking a ride up
and down with the movement of your breath. Keep imagining
this for several minutes, until your breathing becomes slow and
even, and the rising and falling of your diaphragm tapers into a
slight, soothing motion.

2. *Concentrate on in-breath and out-breath.*   Each time your mind
wanders, gently bring it back to the flow of your breath. Be attentive to the peak of your inhalation and to the valley of your exhalation—those momentary gaps when breathing is suspended.

When you have practiced this technique for more than fifteen minutes, your mind will reside entirely in your breath. You
will enjoy the peace that comes as your breathing—this moment-

to-moment miracle that sustains you from cradle to grave—
assumes a graceful, quiet rhythm.

The exercise will make you aware of the accumulated tension in your diaphragm induced by stress. And with this insight
you can catch yourself feeling tense during everyday activities—
driving to work, waiting in line at the supermarket, sitting at your
desk—and measure your anxiety by the way you are breathing. If
needed, you can spend a few minutes watching your breath until
it slows down and becomes even and smooth. So first use your
breathing as a gauge to measure your stress level, then watch
your breath until you feel relaxed.

Recommended Reading

Living Yoga: A Comprehensive Guide for Daily Life edited by
George Feuerstein and Stephan Bodian. New York:
Tarcher/Perigee, 1993.

LIFE AS A MOVIE

Theatre takes place all the time wherever one is.

—John Cage

The average American watches two or more movies each week in
theaters, on video, or on TV. How many movies do you watch?
More importantly, when you watch, how involved do you get?

If you're like most people, movies stir your emotions. When
the scene is sad, you feel sad; when violent, you feel a character's
pain or fear; when sensual, you become aroused; when funny, you
laugh. Now think about this. These are just images on a screen.
Even worse, the images are feigned. People have acted to create
them, or they've been doctored through cinematography. Yet the
images evoke real emotion in you.

Now consider your everyday reality. These images and
events truly happen. Do you respond as easily with the appropriate
emotion, as you do with a movie? Many of us don't. Why? Because

we feel more inhibited. In real life, we're afraid to show too much of ourselves, afraid to show our true emotions.

So, what happens? We miss out. We miss living life to its fullest. We miss meaningful connections with other people. And because our emotions don't match reality, we feel a little less peaceful inside.

What can you do to change? Here's one way: view your own life as a movie. You're probably familiar with the lines from Shakespeare's *As You Like It*: "All the world's a stage, / And all the men and women merely players." You're a player, so get out there and act. Realize that you have a part in life and play it to the hilt. Put every ounce of yourself into it. And enjoy.

Before you step onto the stage of your own life, however, consider this thought from Thornton Wilder: "On the stage it is always *now*; the personages are standing on that razor-edge, between the past and future, which is the essential character of conscious being." Now the curtain goes up. . . .

∞ ∞

Try this:

For seven days, take this life as a drama, perhaps even a comic drama. Think of your whole life as a myth, a story, a play. Even the first time you consider it in that way, doesn't it feel as though a weight has lifted?

It's true. A weight *has* lifted. Now you don't have to take life so seriously. Unfortunately, we all tend to take life too seriously, and unhappiness results. Unhappiness comes from being too serious.

So make your life a game, just a game. Play your part, play it well, but remember you are merely playing a role. In fact, you may have many roles to play: wife, husband, lover, mother, father, friend, employee, employer, and so on. For one week, play each part to the fullest, and remember you're free to be the best father you can be, the best wife, the best lover, or the best friend. After all, it's not the real thing. It's a game. You don't have to take it seriously.

Remember, too, that the game has rules. There are cei. things you can and can't do in any given role, and your conscience knows what these are. So play your part to the fullest but play by the rules. The basic rule is: Don't hurt anybody, physically or emotionally. Beyond that, there are specific rules to help you excel in each role. For instance, if you're a salesperson, you need to put on a smile, present your product in its best light, offer facts, be persuasive, and ask for an order. If you get an order, make the sale; if not, move on. In either case, close with a cheerful thank-you, which in effect says thank you for allowing me to play my role.

Celebrate each of your roles. Be the best you can be and play by the rules; but within the rules, celebrate your part.

If you live like this for seven days, a great weight will lift from you. You will feel peaceful and free. Rather than feeling chained to your roles, you will be happy with them. What's more, this feeling of freedom will last the rest of your life.

WITNESSING

Just let things happen as they do. Let all images and thoughts and sensations arise and pass away without being bothered, without reacting, without judging, without clinging, without identifying with them. Become one with the big mind, observing carefully, microscopically, all the waves coming and going. This attitude will quickly bring about a state of balance and calm.

—*Joseph Goldstein*

Have you ever felt as though you were standing apart from yourself and watching your body? Most of us have had this experience of feeling that we were seeing ourselves through another person's eyes or watching ourselves from afar. And most of us have felt a calm yet detached awareness accompanying this experience.

You can intentionally develop this objective awareness and use it to realize inner peace.

Here's how:

Whatever you are doing, whatever experience or act you are engaged in, watch yourself doing it. When you are eating, watch yourself raise the fork to your mouth. See yourself biting and chewing the food, and then swallowing. Separate each act into its component parts and focus on them, one at a time. When lifting the food to your mouth, see your arm lifting, as if it were the arm of an actor you were directing. As you chew, focus on chewing, on feeling the jaw move with each bite.

Apply this technique to other physical acts you perform during the day. When walking, see your body walking. Intently watch the lift of each leg, the roll of your feet on the ground, the swing of your arms. Do the same when you sweep the floor, vacuum the rug, mow the lawn, or ride a bike. See your body engaged in the physical act by focusing completely on each integral part of it.

It will help if you do things slowly at first. You will then become more aware of each detail of the activity. Be objective, concerned only with lifting, walking, sweeping, chewing— with the exact action and movement of your body during this practice.

What can you expect from it? First, you will notice how much time you spend doing one thing with your body and another with your mind. While eating, for instance, you may be thinking about the business conference you have scheduled for tomorrow or next week. But when you attend to lifting, chewing, tasting, and swallowing, you will harmonize the forces of your mind and your body. This combined awareness integrates your actions. You will become less wasteful with the movement and energy of your body.

Witnessing won't make you leave your body or embark on astral travel. This isn't an occult practice but a simple, practical method for consolidating your mental and physical selves so you can act efficiently and be less distracted by your thoughts.

Don't be scared because this method seems coldly analytic or boring. You won't turn into a robot by witnessing how you move, eat, and breathe. On the contrary, you will become more graceful, more attentive to your physical movements; you'll cultivate something of a dancer's mindfulness as you begin to choreograph your body through the dance of daily life.

Witnessing is a powerful technique for instilling peace of mind. Start with the physical self because it is easier to observe your body than your thoughts and emotions. Once you have a feel for it, you can apply this technique to your mind and your feelings.

Recommended Reading

The First and Last Freedom by J. Krishnamurti. Wheaton, Illinois: The Theosophical Publishing House, 1954.

TECHNOLOGY-ASSISTED PEACE

Business people, athletes, musicians, artists, healers and individuals from all walks of life have used brain wave training to optimize performance and enhance creativity. The benefits that have been reported include reduction of stress and anxiety, increased productivity, increased self-esteem and more joy in day to day living. Some participants have reported new-found feelings of peacefulness, optimism and increased awareness of their spiritual nature.

—Carl Sounder, M.D.

Through brain wave training with a biofeedback machine, you can learn how to relax. What's more, it's fairly easy to do.

Scientists have identified four distinct types of brain waves: beta, delta, alpha, and theta. When you concentrate on something, your mind produces beta, a rapid brain wave. When you are in deep sleep but not dreaming, your brain produces a slow pattern called delta. Between these two, between deep sleep and active thought, are alpha and theta wave patterns. In alpha state, you feel relaxed and alert, and your creative mind is strong. Theta wave patterns mean you are in a deep dream state if asleep or, if awake, you're seeing mental imagery or having an insight.

In many ways, alpha waves have been considered the most significant. When you feel good, your brain produces alpha waves. You generate them when you exercise, meditate, get a restful sleep, or do something creative. When the alpha waves flow, your mind is relaxed.

The original brain-wave training machines, or biofeedback machines, measured alpha waves. When the brain emitted a certain level of alpha, the machine gave a signal. Through this process, people learned how to increase their own alpha output. Furthermore, once they had learned it and practiced it, they didn't need the equipment anymore. They could go into alpha state at will, almost anytime, whenever they needed to relax.

Biofeedback machines can not only help you to increase your alpha waves but to control many of the so-called involuntary bodily functions. For instance, you can learn to raise or lower your heart rate at will, reduce your blood pressure, reduce muscle tension, lower your body temperature, or decrease your nervousness. All of these learned responses are surefire ways to manage stress and increase your sense of well-being. Also, some of the new machines allow you to work with theta waves, which are also deeply relaxing. In fact, some psychotherapists now use theta-control machines in conjunction with therapy to assist individuals with the process of achieving insight.

⚭ ⚭

Options:

Call a few local clinics that offer counseling and psychotherapy, such as mental health clinics or counselors in private practice. Ask if they offer biofeedback sessions. If you want to work with a special kind of biofeedback, such as alpha or theta waves or heart-rate monitoring, ask for that. Find out the costs, and make an appointment.

Another possibility is to buy your own equipment. In the long run, this may be more cost-effective than going to a clinic, plus you'll be able to use the equipment whenever you want. Here's a list of companies that sell biofeedback equipment:

Inner Quest
Kansas City, MO
800-628-MIND

Tools for Exploration
San Rafael, CA
800-456-9887

Pacific Spirit
Forest Grove, OR
800-634-9057

BREAKING LOGIC

However much you knock at nature's door, she will never answer you in comprehensible words.

—*Ivan Turgenev*

Most of us will admit to ourselves that the world around us is incomprehensible. Words cannot describe it.

Indeed, we cannot know the world by thinking about it because our thoughts, like our works, are merely symbols for reality, not reality itself. Here's an example: If someone says to you, "rose," you think of a rose. You have an image of a rose in your mind. But this image will be a composite based on every rose you have ever known.

If someone hands you a rose, you can experience it in reality. You can see it, feel it, smell it. But as soon as you think, "beautiful," the rose disappears. Now the mind enters. The mind begins to categorize this rose by comparing it to other "beautiful" things the mind has known and by making a judgment, "This, too, is beautiful." Even if someone hands you a rose and you think only, "rose," you begin cataloging the present rose as one among many you've known. It is not the same as any you have known, yet you make it so in your mind.

We use our minds to create meaning. The meaning is not really there; the mind generates it. We think up what things mean. We attribute meaning to things by imposing our words or thoughts on them. The rose you were just handed has no meaning. It just is. Why compare it?

By comparing, by trying to find meaning in things, we create a world of trouble. We would be better off following the King's advice in *Alice's Adventures in Wonderland* by Lewis Carroll: " 'If there's no meaning in it,' said the King, 'that saves a world of trouble, you know, as we needn't try to find any.' "

The example of the rose demonstrates how our thoughts do not match reality. Through thinking alone, we lose something, even when we're being logical. But when we're logical, we're thinking clearly, right? That's supposed to be true. Logic helps us do our thinking without making mistakes. It helps us categorize, compare, organize, quantify, and analyze.

Yet logic, though a powerful mental tool, cannot unfold the true nature of the universe. Logic is about the world, it is applied to the world, but it is not the world itself. As Nietzsche said, "There is nothing in reality that conforms strictly to logic."

In fact, the overuse of logic keeps us out of touch with the world. We feel disconnected because our thinking doesn't match reality. Deep inside, we sense that something is missing, that we aren't experiencing things as they are. That's why human beings invented meditation. Many types of meditation have been developed; each helps to clear the mind of thoughts so that we can perceive reality directly.

One type of meditation works strictly on breaking logic. It's called the koan (pronounced in two syllables: *ko' an*), and it comes from the Zen tradition.

A koan is an idea that doesn't make sense to the logical mind. It makes sense on a deeper level. When you meditate on a koan, you seek to find the truth in it. As you do, the logical mind breaks down. When the logical mind is defeated, something else takes over, something that helps to connect you to reality rather than separate you from it.

∞ ∞

Try this:

The following are some traditional Zen koans. Read them over, and note which ones appeal to you.

- The flag doesn't move, the wind doesn't move, only your mind moves.
- Today is the eighth of the month, tomorrow is the thirteenth!
- From where you are, stop the distant boat from moving across the water.
- On top of a flagpole, a cow gives birth to a calf.
- In the trees fish play, in the deep sea birds are flying.
- Who am I?
- What am I?
- (When eating) What is eating?
- (When listening) Who is it that hears?
- (When seeing) Who is seeing?
- (While walking) Who is walking?
- What is my own mind?
- What is the sound of one hand? (You may recognize another wording of this koan—When both hands are clapped a sound is produced: listen to the sound of one hand.)
- What transcends everything in the universe?
- What is my face before my parents were born?

Pick a koan that you especially like. Then meditate on it until you feel a shift in meaning. This may take a few weeks to a few years. Try practicing your meditation in three steps. First, imagine that there is a single, truthful solution to the koan. Second, attempt to state this solution accurately in words. Third, watch the mind's process of knowing break apart as the first two steps become impossible. Ultimately, by following this practice, you'll stop thinking as much and start experiencing things directly.

Recommended Reading

An Introduction to Zen Buddhism by D. T. Suzuki. New York: Grove Press, Inc., 1964.

The Grass Grows by Itself by Bhagwan Shree Rajneesh. Poona, India: Rajneesh Foundation, 1976.

The Three Pillars of Zen by Roshi Philip Kapleau. Garden City, NY: Anchor Books, 1980.

CHAPTER 5

Involving Yourself in Thought

Your mind can make things appear to be the way you want them to be. As Milton put it in *Paradise Lost*: "The mind is its own place, and in itself / Can make a heaven of hell, a hell of heaven." All you need to do is choose which you want. If you think a thought long enough, it becomes reality.

Specific techniques called "affirmation" and "visualization" will help you do this and achieve positive results. This chapter covers both.

Also in this chapter, you'll discover some ways to view the world that will help you feel more connected to it as well as ways to focus on your presence in the world that will help you feel more connected to your inner self. Descartes said, in perhaps the most famous quote in all of history: "I think, therefore I am." It was, for him, the final proof of his existence: the fact that he, himself, was involved in thought. Your thoughts, of course, not only involve you with yourself, but also with the world around you.

AFFIRMING PERSONAL PEACE

Our life is what our thoughts make it.

—*Marcus Aurelius*

If we think a thought often enough, we start to believe it's true. Not only that, but something transforms inside of us to make it come true.

You can try this now. For instance, think, "I accept myself as I am." In reality, most of us don't accept ourselves as we are. Too often, we think only of our problems, our hang-ups, and our sufferings, and this continual negative thinking makes us feel inadequate. So tell yourself, "I accept myself as I am." For this moment, of course, you need to drop all thoughts of the problems you have. Say it again: "I accept myself as I am."

Consider saying this to yourself again and again throughout your day. Now consider saying, "I accept myself," over and over every day for three to four weeks. At that point, your life will change. You will actually feel good about yourself—not all the time, but much more often than you do now. It's remarkable how good you can feel about the person you are simply by using this method.

The method is called "affirmation." An affirmation is a positive statement about yourself that you repeat over and over, until your subconscious gets the message. It's a way to say yes to yourself—a way to change yourself and to help yourself grow.

☙ ☙

Try this:

Choose an affirmation that's right for you and begin to repeat it. Say it silently to yourself. Say it out loud whenever you can. Write it, too. Writing strengthens your inner belief. It's a good idea to write the entire affirmation over and over each day, twenty to thirty times at a sitting.

To get you started, here are some affirmations. You can change the words of any affirmation to make it sound more like you. Select one or two affirmations, and keep working with them until you feel you have made a significant change. It usually takes three to four weeks.

From Physical Health to Inner Peace

- I am good to myself.
- I feel comfortable in my body.
- My body keeps regaining health.
- I feel myself becoming strong.
- My body radiates health.
- My body radiates happiness.

From Love to Inner Peace

- I love my body.
- I am good to myself.
- My body radiates love.
- I can receive love as well as give it.
- I offer the best of myself to others.
- I can connect to the beauty within.
- I forgive myself for mistakes I've made.
- I forgive others for the pains they have caused me.

From Meditation to Inner Peace

- I am free to be myself.
- I am free in this present moment.
- I can drop all thoughts when I meditate.
- I live now.
- I will do only one thing at a time.
- I live my life here in this place . . . now at this moment.
- I can drop desire.
- I can free myself from mental burdens.
- I can free myself from suffering.
- I can't change the past. But I will continue to change myself as I live each moment fully.

From God to Inner Peace

- I am one with God.
- My will is God's will.
- I am an important part of God's plan.
- I am one with the cosmos.
- I am one with the energy source of the universe.
- I see the world as wondrous, and I see myself as an integral part of it.
- I am innocent. I am a child of God. All my desires are holy, and they always have been. (This is from Sondra Ray's book, *Loving Relationships*.)

From Relaxation to Inner Peace

- I am relaxed now.
- I can be still.
- I can relax in the presence of others.
- I open myself to others.

For Peace Itself

- I can find the calm within.
- My life is becoming more and more peaceful.
- I can bathe myself in peaceful feelings.
- I will find greater happiness.
- I feel peaceful within.
- I feel peaceful toward others.
- Whenever I'm feeling tense, I can relax.
- I can surrender myself to deep inner peace.

Recommended Reading

Loving Relationships by Sondra Ray. Berkeley, CA: Celestial Arts, 1980.

VISUALIZING SERENITY

*A rock pile ceases to be a rock pile the moment a single man
contemplates it, bearing within him the image of a cathedral.*
—*Antoine de Saint Exupéry*

Visualization is like fantasizing or daydreaming, only with discipline. You use your mind as a tool to focus your energies. Once you learn this practice, you effectively create your own inner peace, especially if you are the kind of person who loves to fantasize. In fact, your success with this method depends on your ability to imagine.

Try this:

When you are uptight or stressed out or weary from work, how would you most like to relax? It might be by taking a hot bath. It might be by lying beside the ocean and listening to the waves roll in or lying in a mountain pasture in summer. Maybe you'd like to achieve a fantastical body state, such as weightlessness. Whatever it is that you would choose to do, make a note of it.

Then, the next time you feel overworked or full of stress, take a moment to lie down in a quiet room, close your eyes, and let your muscles go limp. Next, picture yourself immersed in that serene scene or state of relaxation that you naturally desired. It's important to select your own image or fantasy rather than adopt someone else's, because the imagination is such a personal affair. So focus on your chosen imagery, including all the nuances, colors, and details that come to mind whenever you think of "getting away from it all."

It may help to write down your "serenity fantasy" and read it over a few times before you shut your eyes and visualize it. Writing it out helps make the imagery more concrete when you do the visualization. Be sure to include plenty of details, unless you are drawn to visions of emptiness or space. And when you visualize yourself in the setting most conducive to your inner peace, see your body lying or sitting comfortably in this environment, which is at a constant temperature just right for you.

You may find that you like to work with more than one visualization or have a different one for each season, especially summer and winter, to balance temperature extremes. This is fine, although it's best to work with one visualization at a time, sticking with it for two weeks to a month. That gives the peaceful images time to penetrate your unconscious mind. Also, if you practice regularly, your peaceful imagery will grow vivid in your mind. However, if you get bored with a visualization, drop it at once and take up a new one.

Finally, remember that the imagery in your serenity fantasies should be as seductive as possible. The more these fantasies captivate your mind, set you in flight, and release you from all other thoughts, the more relaxed you will be.

Recommended Reading

Creative Visualization by Shakti Gawain. New York: Bantam Books, 1982.

SENSING WHOLENESS

You are the world.

—*J. Krishnamurti*

Have you ever thought of yourself as one with the world? Have you ever felt that everything in the universe is interconnected?

In actuality, everything that exists is made up of the same material. The same kind of particles that make up the stars, the earth, and the rocks, also make up all living things. Also, everything is held together by the same kinds of forces. For instance, atomic forces hold small particles close together, while gravity holds large objects close together.

Thus everything that exists, everything in the universe, is intimately connected. When *you* connect with this intimacy, you feel love. After all, what is love but the feeling of connectedness?

For this moment, think of yourself as an essential part of the universe. Think of yourself as a fiber in a strand of a huge, beautifully woven yet ever-changing tapestry. Imagine yourself as one with all that is—whole, complete, connected.

Now ask yourself what usually keeps you from sensing this wholeness. Isn't it your mind and the way your mind normally thinks? Most thinking compartmentalizes, analyzes, categorizes, separates, and segregates. This type of thinking divides you from the whole. Have you heard of "paralysis through analysis?" That's what the brain does. Too often, it paralyzes you by analyzing you and surrounding the world.

You cannot sense wholeness through analysis because the whole is always greater than the sum of its parts. Analysis shows that the whole is exactly equal to the sum of its parts. But this is not true. When adding parts together, something else is created, something the parts didn't have individually. It could be called "togetherness" or "harmony." Your body is really a conglomeration of parts—a brain, a heart, a liver, etc. Each part is useless by itself, but together they work to sustain your life and health. Moreover, as a human being, you are one single yet essential entity intimately connected to a vast cosmic ocean of entities all made up of the same stuff and all held together by the same powerful forces.

∞ ∞

Things to do:

1. *Feeling whole within.* Within yourself, you are whole. To experience this, however, you need to relax your thinking. You need to ignore your incessant stream of thoughts—at least once in a while. When you do this, your thoughts slow down and you become aware of the silence between successive thoughts. In this silence, you can begin to sense the whole.

Try this practice: Use your mind to analyze only when you need to analyze. When you need to categorize, categorize. In other words, use your mind as a helper and use this helper only when needed. When you need to think, think. But relax your mind when thinking isn't necessary. Especially relax your mind when it tries to scold you, make you feel guilty, cause you to worry, or compel you to cling to sad thoughts.

Practice relaxing your thinking every so often throughout the day. In a quiet room, look at a blank, white wall. Identify with the blankness of its surface. This will help relax your mind. Notice how you begin to feel connected when your thinking slows down. The idea of becoming the wall, of joining with the wall, does not work for the logical mind, but it becomes easy as you experience the silent gaps between your thoughts. When you practice this meditation, watch what happens to your sense of wholeness, your sense of connection, and to the love you feel. Relaxing the mind helps you feel better emotionally and become healthier physically.

2. *Feeling part of a larger whole.* When you think about it, the one ultimate truth of the universe is that every creature and thing is part of a larger unity. "Truth is a happening," said the spiritual philosopher Rajneesh, "the final happening, the ultimate happening, in which you dissolve into the whole and the whole dissolves into you."

Meditate on this idea: "You are a drop of water. The universe is the ocean. Since everything is water, you can't distinguish yourself from anything around you. In a sea with billions of drops of water, every drop appears the same." What could be more intimate? You are an essential part of this ocean, and it is an essential part of you.

Or try this meditation: "I am not one thing. I am all things. All that exists in the universe exists in me."

Recommended Reading

You Are the World by J. Krishnamurti. New York: Harper & Row, 1972.

Coming into Harmony by Ilse Klipper. Palo Alto, CA: Pathways Press, 1992.

AWAKENING THE MEMORY

To be able to enjoy one's past life is to live twice.

—*Martial*

You can use your memory in a specific way to instill peace of mind and help you to enjoy a deep, restful sleep when you go to bed at night. This involves an ancient technique that originated in Tibet.

Here's how:

Remember each thing that you did today, in reverse order, from the moment you undressed and got into bed, to the time you woke up in the morning. The following is an example of what might pass through your mind when you do this exercise:

"Put on my pajamas . . . brushed my teeth . . . put the cat out . . . read a book on the living room sofa . . . talked to a friend on the phone . . . ate dinner . . . Cajun shrimp, rice, a salad with creamy Italian dressing . . . came home from work feeling restless and angry . . . finished the report the boss asked for . . . thought how he didn't give me enough time to do it . . . got angry over the deadline and paced the floor of my office . . . had lunch with a co-worker . . . kung pao chicken at the China Delight two blocks from the office . . ." And so on, until the moment you opened your eyes this morning

This practice helps instill peace of mind in a couple of ways. First, by remembering all that you did on a given day, you relive that day in your memory, not only recalling all the things you did but the emotions and thoughts that attended the events. This clears your mind and unburdens you of lingering thoughts. After only one or two nights of experimenting with this technique, you will experience its relaxing effects and, the following morning, feel more rested because the quality of your sleep will have improved.

Second, when you do this exercise, you will discover how much of your day you have forgotten. As you journey through your immediate memory, you'll encounter blocks of time in which you can't remember what you did. When this happens, spend a few moments summoning your recall in order to fill in these blanks. But if you still can't remember what you did, continue with the exercise by going to the next preceding event you can remember. Try to see each of your acts as if you were watching yourself performing them on stage. This will evoke imagery, so you will not remember merely on a verbal level. And with the images that pass across your mind's eye, try to include the mental states and emotions you experienced during each remembered event.

The blocks of forgetfulness are important because they indicate how many of your daily activities you perform unconsciously or with a minimum of awareness. You will be surprised at how much of what you did you can't remember. Of course, this is because you do so many things while thinking about other things. We all spend a good portion of each day not living in the moment at hand, the only time when we *can* live. While talking to a friend, for instance, you may be thinking about what you are going to have for dinner or how good you felt two weeks ago when you were on vacation in Europe. This is why you don't hear three-quarters of what your friend is saying and can't recall the gist of your conversation later on.

So don't be alarmed while doing this memory exercise when you encounter big chunks of time during the day when your body was one place and your mind another. It may be frustrating at first, but if you persist with the practice you'll find that your amnesia will prompt you to be more aware of your daily life because you'll want to remember what you did when you go to bed at night.

By awakening the latent powers of your memory, you will experience a unity of body and mind and become fully engaged in your daily activities. Your focused awareness will give you a reserve of single-minded energy. And you will feel more alive.

Practice this for a few days as you lie in bed, before falling asleep. Soon you'll be able to recall everything you did each day. The sleep that follows will then be deep and dreamless, which is a direct result of having lived your day in the flame of awareness and having remembered the fulfillment that accompanied each of your acts.

CLAIMING YOUR PRESENCE

Mr. Duffy lived a short distance from his body.

—*James Joyce*

Ever feel that you've been "out to lunch" all day long? That is, when you roll into bed at night, you can hardly remember what you did that day. Huge blocks of time are missing and you feel spent and exhausted, as if you left a part of yourself behind, somewhere in time. Or perhaps you recognize your mental absence when you hear a loud sound—the backfire of a car, a sudden shout, a wailing siren. It jolts you awake, aware, alive in your body (albeit with fright), for the first time since . . . when?

Practically everyone has had similar experiences. Why? Because nearly all of us live through each day in a haze, dreaming with our eyes wide open, our bodies in one place and our minds in another. Or else, to save time and be more efficient, we consciously split ourselves by doing two things at once, such as reading the newspaper while eating or talking on the phone while putting away the dishes.

For whatever reason, we spend much of each day in a dreamy, preoccupied state, half attending to our fantasies, half attending to the immediate moment, half alive. This is why we feel frazzled at night in bed when we can't recall how we spent the day. In addition, we tend to feel listless and bored much of the time. That's because we fail to claim our presence in our bodies, in the moment, right now.

☞ ☞

Try this:

Spend one hour living as keenly as possible. For each moment of this hour tell yourself, "I am completely alive and present." Don't say it out loud or repeat it mechanically; that will only distract you. Instead, let the thought, "I am completely alive and present," be a deep affirmation summoning your intensity and passion, and connecting you intimately to each thing you do.

Choose an hour of time when you can move slowly while engaging in physical activities. The important thing is for you to be active—walking, gardening, cleaning the house—for the entire hour. But move much more slowly than usual. When, say, sweeping the floor in slow motion, you will find it easier to claim your presence in your body and remember what you are doing. By moving at half speed, you will assume the grace of a dancer, fusing mind and body, and rousing the energy of awareness.

When the hour is up, take stock of yourself. Do you feel more focused, centered, vibrant, and alive? If so, this method is for you.

Now you can lengthen the time period you've reserved for claiming your presence. You will feel relaxed yet highly energized as you proceed with this practice of being passionately present in the moment, no longer in a daze, no longer missing the miracle of life.

Recommended Reading

Meditation: The Art of Ecstasy by Bhagwan Shree Rajneesh. New York: Harper Colophon Books, 1976.

THE JUGGLING ACT OF THE UNIVERSE

According to particle physics, the world is fundamentally dancing energy; energy that is everywhere and incessantly assuming first this form and then that. What we call matter (particles) constantly is being created, annihilated and created again. This happens as particles interact and it also happens, literally, out of nowhere.

—Gary Zukav

In 1976, physicist Gary Zukav attended a conference for physicists at the Esalen Institute in Northern California. There he met with Al Chung-liang Huang, a tai chi master who was leading a workshop at the conference. Huang told Zukav, "In Taiwan, we called physics wu li [pronounced woo lee]. It means patterns of organic energy." It was then that Zukav decided to write a book titled, *The Dancing Wu Li Masters.*

In fact, since the work of Einstein, physics experiments have proven that the universe is made up entirely of tiny particles, all in constant motion. Not only that, but any particle can, at any moment, change to pure energy—in a sense, disappear. Perhaps even more bizarre, at any moment it may reappear by changing back to a particle again.

What a thought to ponder! The entire universe, at the subatomic level, appears as a dance, a particle dance that continues nonstop. Indeed, each of us is a mass of particles—popping, zipping, zinging—in constant motion, and the same is true of everything around us. The universe itself seems to be a magnificent juggling act, with billions of tiny particles moving all at once, everything whirring continuously, on and on, forever and ever. It's as if there's a party going on. Everywhere—in everything, including ourselves—the particles are dancing.

What does this mean to you as an individual? The particles inside of you bop and bounce as if to music in the cosmic revelry. Even more interesting, the activity within you continues whether or not you participate in it.

Try this:

Why not participate? From this moment on, make a conscious effort to take part in the particle dance of the universe.

Of course, your participation involves a change in perspective, a change in how you see the world. The particle dance is real. The way you see it, however, will be almost completely imagined. So, first look for the real dance, then allow your imagination to take over.

Look around you. With a bright sun above, watch the ripples in some body of water until you see the sun's reflected rays explode into a million tiny points of light. Or, with the sun above, gaze upon some object held within half an inch of your eye and turn this object ever so slightly to reveal a thousand tiny glittering hexagons. Or steadily watch a flickering candle or a burning ember in the fire for five minutes, until it bursts into a thousand tiny dancing dots. Or watch the shimmering brilliance of a sunrise or sunset.

Now, at each of these moments, allow your mind to play. Let the particles in your mind dance in unison with what you see outside yourself. Imagine every particle in your body participating —buzzing, popping, bending, whirring, zinging in the dance.

Let the ripples of microscopic motion fill you from within. Feel this. And feel the happiness unfold.

Recommended Reading

A Brief History of Time: From the Big Bang to Black Holes by Stephen W. Hawking. New York: Bantam Books, 1988.

The Dancing Wu Li Masters: An Overview of the New Physics by Gary Zukav. New York: Bantam, 1979.

The Tao of Physics by Fritzof Capra. Berkeley, CA: Shambhala, 1975.

CHAPTER 6

Using Your Senses to Deepen Serenity

*I*f you watch your thinking for a while, you'll notice that your thoughts about reality seldom match reality. What you know about the world through your senses is closer to the truth. The reason? Through your senses, you experience reality directly. What you see, hear, touch, taste, and smell actually has presence in the world. These things exist.

Yet even though our senses bring us the clearest information about the world, they too can become clouded. When the mind imposes thoughts on what we perceive, our perception changes. What we think we see is often different from what's really there.

After speaking to a crowd that had gathered to hear him, Jesus was asked by a few of his disciples if he thought the crowd understood his message. "Seeing, they do not see," he replied, "and hearing they do not hear." What did he mean by this? He didn't mean that the members of this crowd were literally blind and deaf. He meant that they were missing the point. It was a problem of perception. Because of their preconceived notions, they could not perceive the true nature of reality.

What reality were they missing? They were missing the reality of heaven. As Jesus himself said, "The kingdom of heaven is at hand." Heaven is here now. Simply watch, simply listen. You don't have to wait until you die to experience it. The beauty and the joys of heaven are here for you today. All you need to do is change the way you perceive reality and the doors of heaven will open.

In this chapter, you'll discover numerous ways to use your two major senses, sight and hearing, to experience reality more clearly. These ways of sensing reality, will allow you to penetrate life to its joyous core.

LISTENING

> *Bathe in the center of sound, as in the continuous sound of a*
> *waterfall. Or, by putting the fingers in the ears, hear the sound*
> *of sounds.*

—*Tantric sutra*

Most of us are drawn through our senses to the world outside of ourselves. Indeed our senses seem specifically designed to connect us to things in the world. Rarely do we go inside; we keep moving outward through the senses.

That's why meditation can be so helpful. Through meditation, we go inside. We look behind the senses to find a beautiful and joyous world within.

Hearing allows you to go inside more easily than most meditation techniques. That's because hearing happens on the inside. Sound comes to you from all around and you experience it inside. With sight, you experience the object of vision inside, but you usually feel as though the object is outside of you. With sound, you can close your eyes and feel the sound happening within.

So it's easy to feel as if you're in the center of sound. You always *are* the center of sound. Sound is circular, coming from all directions around you. It comes to you. With sight, you go to it. Sight is linear. It transports you out of yourself: your eyes focus on an object, and bang, you go to the object.

The Tantric sutra leading into this section embodies two methods that will help to free your mind by using sound.

❦ ❦

The methods:

1. *"Bathe in the center of sound, as in the continuous sound of a waterfall."* For a moment, close your eyes and listen. Where do you hear sounds? Don't try to locate the sources of the sounds. Instead, locate your hearing.

This is easiest with a continuous sound such as a waterfall. Try sitting near a waterfall, closing your eyes, and just listening. After a while, you will go deep within your center. The sound itself will continue to move you toward the center. Then, be aware, the sound will begin to blink on and off. You will hear it, then you will have a brief moment when you will hear nothing. This is the true center of sound: silence is at the center. It is the silent point within you that "hears."

All sound is heard by something with no sound, and that is your center. When you go there, you feel peace.

Without a waterfall, you can use music. Of course, by using headphones you can easily feel at the center of sound. But with music, you'll find yourself following notes and these notes will light up spots all over your brain. Look for the center of sound behind the notes. The center will appear in the melody and the harmony created by the notes—in other words, in the composite sound. Listen for music's composite sound, which will lead you to your center.

After you practice this meditation for a while, you can quickly find your center by listening to any set of sounds. Even the sounds produced in the middle of the day on a busy street in the heart of New York City!

2. *"Or by putting fingers in the ears, hear the sound of sounds."* The sound of sounds rests at a still, silent point within you. By plugging your ears to all outside sound, you can hear it. This is a shortcut, a quick way to "hear" the inner silence, a fast journey to the center of your being. Try it. After a few moments you'll feel deeply alone, not lonely but alone—fully alive, fully vibrant, within yourself.

sutra has two parts because these two techniques work ωgether. Both help take you to your center—that ecstatic, peaceful space inside. The first one helps you find your center through sound. The second helps you to hear "the sound of sounds," or soundlessness, which is the center itself.

FROM SOUNDFULNESS TO INNER PEACE

Just by listening deeply, we alleviate pain and suffering.
—*Buddhist saying*

In this section, you'll discover three more techniques using sound. With them, you will make sounds yourself rather than listening to the sounds around you.

ထ ထ

Try this:

1. *Say "mmmmmmm."* Start with deep rhythmic breathing. Then, as you breathe out, keep your mouth closed and intone the *m* sound. This is humming, but you hold a single note: "mmmmmmm."

Intone the sound of *m* each time you breathe out and produce the sound for the duration of your exhalation. The "mmmmmmm" resonates within your mind and your body. Scientists say this one sound creates more internal resonance than any other sound you can make. Try it now and listen.

While humming, it helps to imagine yourself as a hollow reed filling with the sound, resonating with the sound. Imagine yourself gently swaying: "mmmmmmm." Imagine yourself intimately connected to the world: "mmmmmmm."

Try this resonant meditation for fifteen minutes once a day for a week or two. As you do it, watch how peaceful you begin to feel. This particular meditation is said to enhance bodily healing and to help sustain vibrant physical health.

2. *Say "ah."*   Relax yourself with a few deep breaths. Then, on each out-breath, say "ah." Practice this for a while; then begin to drop the *a* in ah, so that, as you breathe out, you pronounce only the sound of *h*. Feel the "hhhhhhh" at the back of your throat. Notice the "hhh" at the end of your breath. This sound will help you to clear your lungs completely.

Use this sound when you feel tense or tired. It's a powerful sound that can reduce your tension and banish your fatigue.

3. *Repeat your own chosen sound.*   Silently or aloud, repeat a sound, a word, or a phrase to yourself over and over in rhythm. Some sounds you can use are: *om, da, zzzzzzz,* or *zoo*. Some possible words are: *one, love, God,* and *sun.* Some phrases are: *peace on earth, on and on, all is one,* and *world without end.* You can also repeat your name. It helps if you synchronize the sounds with your breathing, but the main idea is to use the sound to force all other thoughts from your mind.

To do this, let the sound prevail. Let all other thoughts go. If a thought begins to form, you can use the power of sound to stop it: either increase the volume of the sound or increase your attention to the sound.

When you start using sound in this way, you'll discover that it helps to clear your mind and keep you focused. It rids your mind of distractions. Try it for fifteen minutes each day, and notice how much more peaceful you feel.

SEE THE WORLD AFRESH

The eye sees what it has the means of seeing, and its means of seeing are in proportion to the love and desire behind it.

—*John Burroughs*

When we were children, we were attentive to the world around us. We noticed mud puddles, stones, trees, clouds, and the grain of the hardwood floors in our grandparents' homes. Our eyes were constantly alert to original detail. Because of this, the world was a fascinating place, a garden of sensual delight. It was a mystery to savor, not to solve.

New to the world, we were open to all that it had to teach us. This learning was different from the learning we encountered in school, where we were taught to classify, analyze, and store information in our brains. The kind of learning we experienced when we watched the play of light on a river or the raindrops running down a windowpane educated us in a way that is hard to define, although we look back on those youthful moments nostalgically, often wishing we could relive them. The real joy of our childhood was not so much what we did or where we lived or how many toys we had but the ecstatic pleasure we derived from seeing, hearing, and touching the world with awake senses, in a state of wonder, taking nothing for granted, not even the most commonplace objects.

Do you remember the natural delight you felt as a child? You had mysterious sensations simply standing in the backyard, seeing the grass and birds and flowers, without a thought to spoil the show. At such times, you felt a deep sense of peace; you felt at home in the midst of the ineffable world. You were deeply attuned to your senses, especially your sense of sight. The world was an extravaganza of color—bright, varied, alive. And your best crayoned drawings revealed the one universal quality of children's art: a lucid simplicity that comes from seeing things for the first time.

There are two ways to revive this power for seeing afresh. You will find these techniques helpful and enjoyable, especially if you feel that your perception has become jaded and the world appears drab or monotonous much of the time.

Try this:

1. *Caress the details.*   Whatever you're looking at, experience that object or form fully. Be attentive to its details. If it is a tree, let your eyes roam up and down the trunk and along the branches. If you know what kind of tree it is, let that thought pass across your mind's eye, and then refocus on the actual tree, gazing at its leaves and limbs, aware of the texture and subtle

color changes of its bark. Summon all your energy to your vision. You will then turn the act of looking into the art of seeing.

You can set aside a half-hour or so each day to walk down the street or through the nearest park and practice seeing the world anew. Take your time. Slow down the movement of your eyes to experience each object, each part of the scenery, with unclouded vision.

You can practice this method anytime during the day. For example, you can do it when you suddenly catch yourself staring out your office window and realize that your vision is a blank, that your eyes are merely turned in some direction and not seeing at all. At that moment, bring your attention to your vision and *see* that everyday view you take for granted. Notice the colors of the lawn (so many shades of green!) or the objects on the street, sidewalk, or parking lot as they actually appear.

The great American poet, William Carlos Williams, who conjured beautiful poems out of commonplace objects like sinks and faucets, sheds and wheelbarrows, had a good way of describing this art of seeing. He said, "Caress the details." Let your eyes move lovingly over faces, stones, buildings, or the piece of toast you are about to eat, attending to the minute particulars of the world in which you live. It only takes a few moments, and, for the most part, you can do it without drawing attention to yourself.

2. *Paint with your eyes.*   The second way to practice the art of seeing is based on a method often espoused by painting teachers. It is similar to the detail-caressing technique except that you imagine your eyes are a paintbrush and you are painting the object or scene before you. You paint with your eyes, slowly yet spontaneously letting your vision play over the details that attract your attention. This technique will make you appreciate the ambiance of whatever you are regarding and will awaken you to a world of color and light such as the painter sees.

These two easy and fun methods will go a long way toward reviving that sense of wonder you had as a child. You can choose either method or spend time doing first one, then the other. Experiment to see what works best for you.

Through this practice of seeing afresh, you will no longer feel alienated. You will reengage with plants, animals, people— with the world around you. This brings peace of mind.

Recommended Reading

The Awakened Eye: A Companion Volume to the Zen of Seeing/Drawing as Meditation by Frederick Franck. New York: Vintage Books, 1979.

GAZING

The eye obeys exactly the action of the mind.

—*Ralph Waldo Emerson*

To relax, it often helps to tense yourself. If you've ever attended a class in relaxation, or read a book about it, you may have been asked to tense your entire body, squeeze all your muscles, then let go and relax. This works because by forcing yourself to tense, you feel the extreme opposite of the mental and bodily condition you hope to achieve. A cat knows this instinctively. It will arch its back and stretch its body, then fall into a limp puddle on the living room floor. Sensing one extreme helps you drop into the other.

☜ ☜

Try this:

An ancient gazing technique utilizes this principle. The technique involves staring at an object for thirty to forty minutes without blinking or moving your eyes. You can stare at your face in the mirror; you can stare at a candle or a teacup. The object doesn't matter as much as the single-minded attention you bring to using your eyes. However, you can deepen the effects of this exercise by selecting an object that you find appealing, beautiful, or calming.

Sit comfortably before the object and stare at it continuously for thirty minutes. Try not to move your eyes; try not to blink. This will be difficult at first and your eyes will water. Let them, but try to keep gazing steadily, without blinking. After practicing this technique for a few days, you will find that you can stare for thirty minutes without moving or closing your eyes.

Direct all your energy to your eyes. They will become tense, and you will reach a peak of tension. The moments when you want to blink are the moments to watch out for: your mind is trying to recapture energy to think. Constant gazing is needed because even a single movement of the eyes gives energy to the mind. You can achieve an absolutely fixed gaze with practice. When you are practicing, your thinking will stop as you center your consciousness in your eyes. With your whole mind in your eyes, your mind has no energy left for thoughts.

After doing this for a half hour, close your eyes. Let them relax, and your mind will fall effortlessly into a deep relaxation. From the climax of tension, the opposite will happen spontaneously. You will feel serene.

Remember to end each session by closing and relaxing your eyes, and take time to enjoy the ensuing mental tranquillity.

SHIFTING FOCUS: FROM THE OUTSIDE IN

Look upon some object, then slowly withdraw your sight from it,
then slowly withdraw your thought from it. Then.

— *Tantric sutra*

All our lives we tend to move outward, into the world; rarely do we move inward, toward ourselves. It's natural to move outward. We need things outside of ourselves. We need food, water, shelter, clothing, and other goods, so we need to work to make money for purchasing these things.

Understanding the world, and moving into it, is crucial to our survival. Hence we tend to focus almost exclusively on what's happening outside of ourselves. That means we lose sight of what's happening inside. We hardly ever bother to move inward, and now, when we try, we tend to lose our way and struggle to find the center. We have lost touch with our inner core.

What will you find at the inner core? Peace. The deepest, happiest peace you can know is there, close at hand, waiting. It's just below the surface, and once you have practiced moving inward, you can find it.

It's not hard to do this. But you need to take some time to learn how. As easily as you learned to move outward into the world, you can learn to move inward to your center. That's what this sutra is all about.

∽ ∽

Try this:

Look upon some object. Pick an object you enjoy, something that pleases you visually—a flower, a face, some dearly cherished possession. It's better to select something simple in its features. Now look upon it. Drink it in with your eyes. Become one with it. Notice the point of vision where you become one with this object, the point at which you merge. Notice that this point feels as if it's outside of you. Is it? Your eyes are at one with the object.

Slowly withdraw your sight from it. The image of this object is impressed on your sight. Now slowly close your eyes while keeping the image strong in your mind. Visualize it fully. The image is now a thought in your mind. The object has become a thought. Where is this thought? It's near your sense of sight, at the surface of your mind, on the tip of your brain—somewhere just between your vision of the object itself and your deep inner core.

Slowly withdraw your thought from it. While keeping your eyes closed, allow the image of this object to dissolve. Carefully but purposefully, let the thought dissolve until all you "see" is a blank screen. Then, as the image disappears, go deeper and deeper, to an undisturbed center, a place behind the thought, a place behind all thought. Here, you are in a windless place where no thought stirs.

Then. At this calm center, then. . . . Quietly, you become one with inner peace at this deepest place within. There exists no thought, no symbol, simply a feeling of imperturbable calm. Now you are at one with yourself, as completely as you were at one with the object in your vision a few moments ago.

CHAPTER 7

Time

*B*y dwelling in the past or anticipating the future, we miss the moment. Yet this very moment is the only time in which we can live.

In fact, the present moment is eternal. It is always "now." The present moment—a moment with no past and no future—exists outside of time. It explodes with the immediate magnificence of all that is, of all that's happening now. And now. And now!

Why do so many of us miss the moment?

BOOM IS THE SHOCK OF EACH NEW INSTANT

Boom is the shock of each new instant that you realize you're still alive.

—*Tennessee Williams*

In Tennessee Williams's play, *The Milk Train Doesn't Stop Here Anymore*, the main character, a rich elderly woman named Sissy Goforth, is close to death although she doesn't know it. She is busy writing her memoirs when she is paid an uninvited visit from a man who says he knows her. She learns that this man, over the past few years, was with many of her friends when they died and he has become known in social circles as the "Angel of Death." This gives her a start, and she begins to wonder if she might be the next to go.

What ensues, however, appears to be a guided medi
with the Angel of Death helping Sissy to live in the p
moment. His favorite word is *boom*. He says it every so often as if
he wants the present moment to explode. He describes boom as
waves crashing on the shore, each wave creating a new moment, a
new boom.

Boom: each moment explodes into possibility. Boom: life
becomes fresh. Boom: death has not happened yet. Death becomes
a minuscule event in the faraway future. In the play, Chris (the
"angel") says, "Death is one moment, and life is so many of them."

The message: Live now. Seize the moment.

You can shock yourself into living in the present moment.
Contemplating your own death is one way. Living dangerously is
another. If you're climbing on a mountain face or jumping from an
airplane, you'll likely pay attention to each specific moment. Certain rides at amusement parks can scare you into embracing the
present moment with all your vitality.

But what can you do when you can't startle yourself into
living in the present moment? You can pay attention. You can
attend to the details of the moment. The first way is powerful, the
second way is subtle.

∽ ∽

Try this:

Consider that you have only one moment: this moment. If you
miss it, you miss everything. Now, here are two ways to keep
your attention in the present moment.

1. *The thought of death.*   When people are dying, when they
know they have only a few months or a year left of life, they
learn to live now. Very quickly, their perspective changes. Each
moment becomes precious. One meditation based on this is to
live this day as if it were your last. Live today as though you will
die tomorrow. It may even be true. You may die tomorrow or
you may die later today. Allow this possibility to change your
perspective now.

2. *Act spontaneously.*   Your main purpose is to keep your attention on what you're doing in the present moment. So how can you remain totally attentive to the moment? Be impulsive. Allow no thought to enter; think no thought whatsoever. When you act, act instinctively from your true nature, and when you react, react instinctively to what's happening around you. When with others, show your heartfelt feelings without hesitation.

Consider for a moment how you are when you become thoroughly involved in an activity. You lose yourself in it. Two hours from when you began you realize that you have been completely immersed. If you're lucky enough to love your job, this can happen at work. Often it will happen when you get involved with your favorite hobby or a creative activity such as drawing or writing. It can also happen when you're meditating or when you're doing physical exercise. How can you lose yourself in an activity? By paying attention. You become so vigorously involved that you give the activity your complete attention. In other words, you do nothing each moment but act or react. From now on, whenever time passes like this for you, whenever you get so absorbed in an activity that you lose yourself in it, take notice of what you're doing. You can learn from it. You can apply the same passionate attention to anything you do.

Here's one final idea from *The Milk Train Doesn't Stop Here Anymore*: "Life is all memory, except for the one present moment that goes by you so quick you hardly catch it going." Pay attention. Catch each moment as it goes by.

WHEN TIME DOESN'T MATTER

Peace is when time doesn't matter as it passes by.

—*Maria Schell*

When you live in the present moment, time disappears. Without distractions, fully occupied with what you're doing, you don't notice time as it passes by. You come alive this very minute, and a

peaceful feeling settles deep within. But most of us have ti
centering our attention on only what's happening now. Mem
of past events or anticipations of future possibilities cloud ...ie
present.

So here you have a hint about this technique. If you can make
time disappear, you immediately enter the present, actively living
now, feeling serene about yourself and the world. When you can
drop all memories of the past and anticipations about the future,
the present moment becomes vast and encompassing.

How does this help you to achieve inner peace? It removes
the distractions of the past and the future that keep you from
enjoying yourself now.

Consider how time and thought work. Many things are
always happening, inside of you and all around you. At any given
moment, you can attend to them. On the other hand, you can
spend time remembering something you did two weeks ago. Or
you can think ahead about some event scheduled for next Monday.

It happens just by thinking. You lose the moment as soon as
thoughts form about the past or future. What's worse, if you react
emotionally to your thoughts, you travel further from the present.
For instance, when recalling a past event, you may feel sadness,
guilt, or shame—the most common negative emotions associated
with memories. When pondering a future event, you may feel
anxiety, worry, or fear—the most common negative emotions
about the future. You may even experience thoughts about the past
and the future together, for instance, when you feel guilt over
something you did in the past and begin to worry that it might
happen again.

Let's say your mind is on some sadness you experienced two
years ago and now you meet someone new. Right off, the sadness
gets in your way. You say hello but you look down. You frown. Your
conversation is short, and the other person moves on. You missed
that person. By dragging the weight of your past around, you
stopped living in the present; you missed something that could
have been enjoyable. Ultimately, you let someone get away who
could have been a new friend.

On the other hand, you may be living in the future. Let's say you're feeling anxious about some place you have to be in twenty minutes. You meet another new person. This time you say hello, but you wrinkle your brow, you appear nervous, you look at your watch, and even though you could talk for ten minutes and still make your appointment with time to spare, you say, "Well, it was nice meeting you," and move on in a hurried manner.

You can see how easy it is to lose the present moment. How can you regain it?

∞ ∞

Try this:

To get into the spirit of this method, consider the following idea from Lin Yutang: "A good traveler is one who does not know where he is going to, and a perfect traveler does not know where he came from."

When you begin to identify your thoughts about the past and future, you can recognize how they change your mood in the present. No matter what you do for the next week, watch your thoughts. What are you thinking? How often are your thoughts about something in the past or the future? How strong is the emotional attachment to each of these thoughts? Usually the stronger your *negative* emotional attachment to a thought, the more it removes you from the present moment.

Now, for another week, practice dropping all thoughts about the past and the future. Let your mind get tough. Tell the intruding thought, "I don't want you here now. *I* want to be here now." Prevail over the distracting thought. As you do, you emerge into the present.

Notice that when you drop the thoughts, the emotions attached to them drop, too. You are left free and clear to feel the world firsthand.

Recommended Reading

Be Here Now by Ram Dass. New York: Crown Publishers, 1971.

BECOMING ONE WITH CHANGE

Nothing is permanent but change.

—*Heracleitus*

When you stop to think about it, you'll realize that everything in this world is changing. In fact, the only permanent feature is change. People, animals, and plants grow and die each day, and the earth itself, with its oceans, rivers, and mountains, slowly yet ceaselessly changes. Every cell in your body (except nerve cells) is replaced by a new cell every seven years, and time holds still for no one—not even you.

This last perception may seem a bit frightening at first, but it confirms that change is the underlying reality of life on this planet. Knowledge of this can save you a great deal of stress and sorrow. By accepting the transitory nature of life, you begin to appreciate the world as it is, in constant flux, and yourself as but one small yet integral part of the unending transformative process. Consequently, you can accept life as it is and not as you think it should be.

Such a perspective can further your quest for inner peace. Instead of clinging to pleasure and striving to avoid pain, you will start to accept them as transitory experiences that will happen, regardless of how hard you struggle to make your life a bed of roses. While you can't change the nature of life, you can change your response to it by accepting the inevitable sorrows and tragedies you encounter in the same spirit with which you accept the pleasures and joys. Through this spirit of acceptance, you can embrace an inner peace that cannot be shaken or destroyed by life's ever-changing reality.

CO CO

Try this:

The next time you find yourself facing an unpleasant event, a trying time, or a sudden sorrow, tell yourself, "This too will pass." You needn't say the words out loud, especially if that would be inappropriate to the occasion. Nevertheless, take stock of the experience and tell your mind, "This too will pass." Let that thought resonate within you as an affirmation, and then proceed to make the best of the situation at hand. In this way, you won't lose your inner calm when you face life's trials and tribulations.

To succeed with this practice of remaining calm regardless of circumstances, remind yourself of transitoriness in the same manner when an unexpected and fortunate surprise comes your way. In the midst of your sudden happiness over the event, say to yourself, "This too will pass," and then go about celebrating your good fortune.

Cultivating this attitude loosens your attachment to the roller coaster ride of life, with all its ups and downs. Eventually, your emotional self will no longer depend on things "turning out your way." Life doesn't exist to meet your expectations; so why should you pin your expectations on life? Using this method of acknowledging the passage of events helps you to drop your expectations and greet your unraveling destiny with a deep inner calm.

Recommended Reading

The Wisdom of Insecurity: A Message for an Age of Anxiety by Alan Watts. New York: Pantheon, 1951.

RECALLING A PLEASANT MOMENT

You're never too old to have a happy childhood.

—*Tom Robbins*

Do you have fond memories? Think about your past for a minute. Can you remember a time when you felt the world was beautiful and full of splendor? Or when you felt intense love? Or connected to everything around you? Or absolutely calm and safe?

Recall this time again. Watch what happens when you think about it. If you recall the past event vividly, your feelings will return. You will experience the same intense and beautiful feelings right now, as if the event were happening all over again. Perhaps that's what James Montgomery meant when he said, "Remembered joys are never past."

Obviously, as you think about some past event, your mind wanders. This is called reverie or reminiscence. You leave the present mentally, yet you become grounded in the moment through your feelings. The present moment is lost in part, but in this case it's worth it to release such strong and sublime emotions as love, safety, joy, or peace.

You have probably heard about the power of positive thinking. Well, this single effective technique will help you think positively and make use of the attendant power. For instance, when you recall one of your favorite moments from the past, you begin to feel stronger and more capable in the present. When you recall something you did well in the past, the feeling that helped you then can help you now.

It follows that you can use this technique in two ways: to enjoy the present moment or to help you succeed at something you're currently doing.

☙ ☙

Here's how:

First, search your life for important moments. Think about small chunks of time that mattered to you. As Cesare Pavese said, "We do not remember days, we remember moments." Consider childhood events as well as any precious moments that may have happened last week.

Select one of these moments when everything seemed right, a moment that was profoundly delightful. Then allow yourself to enjoy a fond memory. Go into the memory to the point where you experience the event again. Remember all that was happening and all you were feeling. Absorb it completely. Now stay in the feeling. Bask in it, and let that feeling glorify you again. At this point, you've reconnected with something strong and beautiful that's deep inside of you. Use the power of this connection to energize you in the present moment.

PART THREE

Emotional Peace

Every moment of resistance to feeling armors our heart.
                                                    —*Stephen Levine*

*H*ow do you feel about the world? How does the world affect you? How do you get along with others? It is through your emotions that you connect with other human beings and with the world around you.

Your emotions bring you laughter and feelings of love and joy. But your emotions also bring you sadness, anger, and despair. Perhaps, like many of us, you experienced threatening or frightening events when you were a child, often as the result of an adult's thoughtless or abusive actions. And now when you recall these painful events, you feel yourself armoring your heart and resisting close relationships with other people.

We were all wounded in the process of growing up, and when others caused these wounds, we learned to armor our hearts, to protect ourselves from more emotional hurt. As adults, we often involuntarily resort to this defense mechanism when it is not appropriate and thus block ourselves from experiencing our true feelings and from showing them to others.

Yet our relationships with others work best when we show how we feel. The quality of marriages and friendships hinges on this. Therefore it is important to be emotionally honest, to express our feelings without abusing others or ourselves. Without emotional honesty, we can never be at peace with ourselves. By accepting our emotions, we can begin to heal the pain caused by the abuses inflicted on us.

The methods in this section will help you to get in touch with your uplifting, positive emotions and to detach from emotions that are obsessive. You'll learn how to use your assertiveness, imagination, and creativity to deepen your sense of peace. Moreover, you will learn how the media, cultural conditioning, and excessive desires affect you adversely, and how you can free yourself of their negative effects.

In addition, you'll strengthen two of your most vital emotional connections in life: humor and love.

CHAPTER 8

Making Connections

*T*oday there is much talk about "the fear of intimacy," which is actually a fear of making connections. Many psychologists claim that this is one of the biggest fears human beings face. Usually when we hear "fear of intimacy," we think of the fear that arises between lovers or potential lovers. Yet our fear of intimacy can be a fear of connecting with ourselves. If we resort to *Webster's*, we see that *intimate* means "essential" as well as "belonging to or characterizing one's deepest nature."

How often do we respond to the world of people and things around us in a way indicative of our deepest nature? For most people, the answer is rarely, because we're so afraid of intimacy. If we show our inner selves to the world, we then become intimate with the world.

Perhaps many of us fear intimacy because it is a challenge, and it is easier to resist a challenge than to face it. Facing a challenge requires work and effort. Yet only by facing the challenges in life can we grow.

If we are afraid of intimacy today, isn't it because it is one of the greatest challenges we face in life? Meeting this challenge can produce a wealth of possibilities to make our lives more fulfilling.

The pleasure of intimacy may be the most gratifying experience we can have, as it connects us with other human beings, with our own inner selves, and with the world around us. The fulfillment of intimacy is the fulfillment of our own deepest nature. Through intimacy, we can express our emotions without being hung up on what others think of us. And through intimacy we understand, welcome, and appreciate other people.

   This chapter will teach you ways to assert yourself when confronting unpleasant situations and people who knowingly or unknowingly try to take advantage of you. You will learn to use your imagination and creativity to express your emotions and deepen your sense of intimacy with yourself and with the world. You will also learn methods for using your senses to celebrate nature, your work, and other people in ways that will bring you peace.

ASSERTING YOURSELF

Nothing is unthinkable, nothing impossible to the balanced person.
                                                        —*Lewis Mumford*

When dealing with other people, do you remain emotionally balanced? Most of us don't. We overreact or underreact much of the time. What happens when we respond to others this way? Our stress level increases.

   On one extreme, you may overreact. You may blow up too often, yell and scream, or behave with hostility in order to get your way. On the other extreme, you may underreact. In this case, you let other people take advantage of you. You become silent or overly agreeable, or you simply let others have their way too often.

   When you act at either extreme, tension builds. Also, the emotional life in your relationships will seem distorted or incomplete. In one case, you force too much of yourself on others. In the other case, you give up too much of yourself.

   But there is a middle ground. In your relationships, your behavior can be both socially appropriate and emotionally fulfilling. This middle ground is like Baby Bear's porridge in the story of the Three Bears: it's not too hot and not too cold. It's just right.

Acting from this center ground is called assertive behavior, while the extreme stances discussed above are called "aggressive" and "passive" behavior, respectively. The more you act from the standpoint of moderation in your relationships, the better you will feel. Assertive behavior means sticking up for your rights and protecting your needs without overdoing it. It means you don't let others push you around nor do you push others around to get your own way.

Let's look at an example.

Situation: You're waiting in a long line at the grocery store or at the movies. Someone butts in line ahead of you.

Aggressive response: You get mad, your temper rockets, and you yell, "Hey, get out of here! Get back at the end of the line where you belong!" After an incident like this, your anger and tension stay high for a long time.

Passive response: You don't say a thing. You get mad but keep it inside. Soon you are mad at yourself for being such a pushover, for letting people get away with such things. Meanwhile, your tension and internal stress remain high for a long time after the incident.

Assertive response: You approach the person and say in a normal tone, "I know you must be in a hurry, but we were all waiting for a long time before you got here. Please go to the end of the line and wait your turn like everyone else." With this response, you remain levelheaded. You do something to solve the problem. When you are sensible and calm, even if the other person wants to argue, he or she will look like a fool.

You will confront numerous situations every day that call for assertive behavior. A cashier may shortchange you, a waiter may bring you the wrong order, someone may jump through the door of the taxi you just hailed. These situations happen among strangers, but the most serious situations transpire among friends, especially intimate friends. With close friends, one person may yell to get his or her way, another person may give in all the time. This is common. Yet these relationships remain immature. They do not grow because they lack fairness. When people bully each other or allow themselves to be bullied, the relationship feels incomplete.

Which kind of person are you? Are you passive or aggressive? How can you become assertive?

∞ ∞

Try this:

You can easily learn to do this practical technique on your own. First, write your assertive responses to the following situations. Practice saying them to yourself. Then, practice these responses when actually confronted by the situations.

- Your neighbor is playing music too loud.
- You are taking a friend to a meeting. When you arrive at your friend's house, he or she keeps puttering around so that you will arrive late.
- After you have adopted a healthy diet, a friend offers you candy or cookies.
- You're using one of your favorite techniques to achieve peace of mind. An old friend sees you and makes fun of you because you look a little silly; he or she tries to get you to stop.
- Write down a disruptive situation in which you typically become too aggressive or too passive. (Now what's your assertive response to this situation?)

Remember, assertiveness is another way to reduce stress and strengthen your connection to inner peace.

Recommended Reading

Anger Kills: Seventeen Strategies for Controlling the Hostility That Can Harm Your Health by Redford Williams, M.D. and Virginia Williams, Ph.D. New York: Times Books, 1993.
The Anger Workbook by Lorraine Bilodeau, M.S. Minneapolis: CompCare Publishers, 1992.

When I Say No I Feel Guilty by Manuel J. Smith, Ph.D. New York:
    Bantam Press, 1975.
Your Perfect Right: A Guide to Assertive Living by Robert Alberti, Ph.D.,
    and Michael L. Emmons, Ph.D. San Luis Obispo, CA:
    Impact Publishers, 1990.

SENSING WITH THE HEART

Without the heart, the essential is invisible to the human eye.
                                        —*Antoine de Saint Exupéry*

If you have a deeply emotional nature and respond to the world
around you primarily by feeling rather than thinking, then you
have a ready means to inner peace through your senses. All you
need to do is put your heart into a sensory experience. This involves a simple and pleasurable practice that will bring you serenity
as well as appreciation for the miraculous nature of your body.

◌ ◌

Here's how:

Envision an inner pathway from your eyes to your heart. Imagine
that your sense of vision has roots that extend to your heart. Now
look around. Whatever object you see, feel that you are seeing it
with your heart.

To succeed with this method, it helps to practice in a natural setting—a backyard, meadow, woods, or park—or in a
room furnished with things you care for, such as photographs
of a loved one, prints of your favorite paintings, a tapestry that
pleases your eye, a vase of tulips, or some potted geraniums.
Choose whatever setting pleases you most, so that you can tap
the well of love in your heart.

Once you settle yourself in the environment you've chosen,
slowly look around, letting your vision dwell on each object.
Take time to notice all the details. Let your gaze be soft and
inviting. Imagine the presence of the plant, the tree, the picture

—anything you see—entering your body through your eyes and settling in your heart. Lovingly contemplate what you see and feel the awakened warmth and generosity of your heart. Let your response to the world around you be deeply emotional. Center it in the region of your heart, not your head. You might even try placing your hand on your chest to focus the source of your perception.

By spending a few minutes each day sensing with your heart, you will instill in yourself a love energy that is relaxing and satisfying. In turn, you will be more aware of the beauty around you. Notice how this energy sensitizes your eyes and nourishes your vision.

You will probably find it easiest to start with the sense of sight because it is usually the predominant sense. But if you are visually impaired or practice a profession that relies on one of your other senses (such as music, massage, or even wine tasting), you can apply this method to that well-developed sense. You'll turn tasting, touching, smelling, or listening into emotionally gratifying experiences.

If you have an emotional or sensuous orientation to life and a vivid imagination, this method can work wonders for you. Let it open your heart to the world.

Recommended Reading

Listening with the Heart: And Other Communication Skills by Sara Bhakti, Ph.D. Santa Cruz, California: Gaea Center, 1991.

THE SONG OF YOURSELF

There is delight in singing, though none hear
Beside the singer.

— Walter Savage Landor

Many of us don't sing because we think we can't carry a tune. While this may be true from a musical standpoint, singing, like loving, is its own reward. Singing can make you merry. So forget about how you sound. If you give up your self-consciousness and embarrassment, the practice of singing may open the door to your heart.

Not everyone can be an opera or rock star. But nearly all of us can sing, especially when we have a reason to feel good or have something to celebrate.

Burst into song when you're in a good mood, and you'll heighten that mood and enjoy yourself even more. Also, if you do this on a regular basis, you will begin to associate singing with feeling good, and you'll sing at opportune times of the day, regardless of your mood.

∞ ∞

Try this:

Sing. Sing without any thought of yourself. Just let it happen. The proverbial shower is a good place to start. As you feel the cleansing sense of well-being that comes from hot water spilling over you, and as you lavish your body with soap and shampoo, you have every cause to sing.

Don't think about how you sound. Don't worry if your tone is off-key. Don't be concerned if you forget the words after the start of the song—make them up as you go along! Free-associate, supply your own lyrics, fill in the gaps with pure nonsense, but sing. Keep belting out your own melody.

Sing your favorite songs, songs that you hear on the radio, or songs that you remember from the happiest times of your childhood. Cut loose with verve and gusto amid the rising steam of the shower. Sing as though singing to an audience of close friends who accept you for the person you are, with all those quirks, imperfections, and foibles that make you so wonderfully human.

Singing is both cathartic and celebratory. If you take time to sing each day—whether in the shower, driving to work, with a friend, or alone in your room—you will relieve yourself of many worries and cares, and become more cheerful.

THE EVER-LIVING PRESENCE OF THE COSMOS

There is an impulse still within the human breast to unify and sanctify the total natural world—of which we are.

—*Gregory Bateson*

Today the word *humility* has negative connotations. We often associate this quality with a lack of self-assertiveness or self-esteem. Many of us share the notion that a humble person has a martyr complex and is willing to sacrifice his or her needs in order to please others. True humility, however, has nothing to do with self-sacrifice but comes from knowing that one is a small yet integral part of all life.

If you examine the biographies of individuals who have possessed the intellect or the compassion to perform seeming miracles —people such as Einstein, Gandhi, Albert Schweitzer, and Mother Teresa—you will see that they have one thing in common: a deep appreciation for the mystery of life. Einstein said, "The most beautiful thing we can experience is the mysterious. It is the source of all art and science."

One of the most moving experiences you can have in life is a feeling of reverence for the powers that animate the universe. This might sound abstract or a little too "cosmic" to be practical, yet the joy of this experience lies in savoring the mystery of the universe without trying to solve it. You avail yourself of this grand experience when you realize you are intimately connected with the mystery. To have this realization is to become humble in the true sense of the word. You stop thinking that you are the be-all and end-all of existence. You stop obsessing over personal problems. You begin to see all the people, animals, plants and things around you, and realize that each has an existence, a life of its own, independent of your life. At the same time, you will feel the interrelatedness of everything you see, in all of your surroundings.

This feeling of interconnectedness can bring you to your senses. You will stop sleepwalking through life. You will feel rooted, at home wherever you go, and less dependent on external circumstances to dictate your state of mind.

In short, sensing the ever-living presence of the cosmos will humble you with a growing appreciation of the vastness, the wonder, and the mystery of the world outside your skin. This is the same humility felt by artists, scientists, and philanthropists who have enriched our planet. It will help you to become more aware of living each moment and of making the most of each day. This is the humility of the great painter Goya, who said at the end of his life, "I am still learning." When you sense the essence of earth, trees, stars, sun, birds, and sky, you become a learner again, open to life's greatest mysteries.

☙ ❧

Try this:

Set aside a time period, at least one week, during which you will attune yourself to the rhythms of the earth. Each day, get up just before dawn, go outside, and watch the sun rise. Breathe the early morning air, gaze at the horizon and the sky as the sun ascends and disperses the night. If you live in a congested metropolitan area where you can't see the sunrise, sit quietly in your room, without any lights on, and watch the slow, subtle emergence of light as the new day begins.

Do the equivalent in the evening. Watch the sunset, the twilight, the first stars coming out. Go to a natural area or the nearest park, and be still; open yourself to the phenomena of dawn and dusk. You will soon feel the meditative stillness during these two times of the day as you connect with the rhythm of the earth.

During this trial period, spend as much time outside as you can, observing the sky, stars, birds, trees, flowers, lakes, streams, and other natural objects. Remain receptive; invite the vast mystery of life into your being. If you live in a city, you can still look up and see a patch of sky. Your attitude is what matters. Think of yourself as a vital part of the endless universe; let this thought go deep inside as you look about, as you listen to the birds and the wind, as you gaze at the moon and stars.

At the end of each of your walks or the times you spend greeting the dawn and dusk, close your eyes to silently bless the vastness of universe. Bless your own body, and appreciate its growing sensitivity to the mysterious powers of life.

Take stock of how you feel at the end of each week you set aside for this experiment. Are you more relaxed and in tune with the day? Do you have greater peace of mind? Are you feeling less complacent and more reverent toward life?

Recommended Reading

Dharma Gaia: A Harvest of Essays in Buddhism and Ecology edited by Allan Hunt Badiner. Berkeley, California: Parallax Press, 1990.

Earth Prayers from Around the World: 365 Prayers, Poems, and Invocations for Honoring the Earth edited by Elizabeth Roberts and Elias Amidon. San Francisco: Harper Collins, 1991.

Earth Wisdom by Dolores LaChapelle. Silverton, Colorado: Finn Hill Arts, 1978.

The Norton Book of Nature Writing edited by Robert Finch and John Elder. New York: W. W. Norton, 1990.

IMAGINE EMBRACING EVERYONE YOU MEET

Darkness may hide the trees and the flowers from the eyes but it cannot hide love from the soul.

—*Kahlil Gibran*

In our society it is not always appropriate to hug someone, especially if you are meeting that person for the first time. You either shake hands (a greeting which Leo Buscaglia calls "distancing"), or say hello, nod, and don't touch at all. Hence greeting and meeting people often has a perfunctory quality, and many of us feel a certain coldness, embarrassment, or self-consciousness when making someone's acquaintance. Numerous introductions and encounters seem superficial because the people involved exchange quick smiles before averting their eyes.

By engaging yourself in the following method, you can generate a relaxing sense of warmth and acceptance when meeting others.

∞ ∞

Try this:

The following method is similar to "Emanate Peace with Others," a method in the next section. Both are especially suited to emotionally oriented people.

The next time you meet someone for the first time, or greet a person playing a professional role (such as your boss or an insurance agent), look into the person's eyes and imagine giving him or her a warm embrace. Take as much time to imagine this as you would to actually embrace the person. At the same time, don't be gushy. A simple hello or "how are you?" is sufficient. Smile and let your gaze be soft and inviting as you look into the person's eyes.

This act cuts through the nervousness and feelings of alienation we often associate with meeting people. You will really see the human being before you and welcome his or her presence. This individual will in turn feel the warmth of your greeting and relax in your presence. Of course, this may not happen in every case, but it will happen enough for you and others to feel good about it. Moreover, you will radiate peace, joy, and confidence in social situations.

Recommended Reading

Love by Leo Buscaglia. New York: Fawcett Crest, 1972.

EMANATE PEACE WITH OTHERS

A loving person lives in a loving world. A hostile person lives in a hostile world: everyone you meet is your mirror.

—*Ken Keyes, Jr.*

Most likely you are aware of how other people affect you. You may frequently find yourself in the company of someone who is a drain on your energy. He or she may be boring or irritating, yet the social situation is such that you can't just walk away. Afterward, when you are by yourself, you feel tense, angry, or restless. It's as though you were a chameleon and colored yourself, with all of that person's annoying traits. And, in fact, that's exactly what you did.

Unless you are a hermit, life in this world forces you to deal with other people, some of whom you will find distasteful and provoking. While you can't control the people you encounter, you *can* decide how they affect you.

∞ ∞

Here's how:

The next time you are with someone, go within yourself for a moment and be still. Then, from deep inside, summon the feeling of peace and radiate it silently to that person. Feel: "Peace be with you." Don't just say it to yourself, *feel* it. When you do this with someone you like, it can arouse joy.

You can also do this with someone you find particularly tiresome. When you emanate peace, you take control of the situation. By summoning your own measure of inner peace and projecting it, you will feel in command of all the negative feelings you associate with certain people. Then you can sit calmly with them and listen to their tedious talk without being bothered, since you are responding with your own communication. You are "getting a word in edgewise" in a way that's conducive to mental peace.

As you practice this, don't be surprised if you see a change in the person before you. Your thoughts have power, and you are using the power in a concentrated fashion by projecting your inner peace onto this person. If he or she suddenly becomes calmer, less restless, and less disposed to bowl you over with talk, you can inwardly rejoice in the effects of your practice. But even if your emanation of peace has no appreciable effect on the person, it will still work wonders in helping *you* remain free of stress in unpleasant social situations.

Recommended Reading:

Compassion in Action by Ram Dass and Mirabai Bush. New York: Bell Tower, 1992.

THE CREATIVE TOUCH

We have no art—everything we do is art.

—*Balinese saying*

Each and every one of us is creative. Yet we impose a great limitation on ourselves with the belief that only certain people are creative. We call these people "gifted" or "talented" because of their abilities to paint, write, compose music, play an instrument, or excel in some other artistic pursuit. Unfortunately, when we take this point of view, we then believe that we are noncreative if we lack the ability or inclination of the painter, sculptor, or poet. We may compare ourselves with professional artists and decide we do not measure up to the standards of art galleries, publishing houses, musical bands, or orchestras. We tend to dismiss the "artistic touch" as a wonderful capability we had as children but can never re-experience fully because we didn't continue those flute or painting lessons or because we didn't graduate with a degree in fine arts.

A few special individuals, we are told, are inspired by the Muse. The rest of us are fated to be nothing but *consumers* of art. We will decorate our houses with other people's paintings, play other people's songs on our stereos, and read other people's published journals, poems, and stories. As a professor tells a despondent college student in Matt Groening's comic strip "School Is Hell": "The sooner you all face up to the fact that you are lazy, untalented losers, unfit to kiss the feet of a genius like Friedrich Nietzsche, the better off you'll be."

Do you remember the finger paintings and crayon drawings you made as a child? And do you remember the quiet, satisfying fun you had when you made them? Nearly all of us can recall being artists as children, with fresh vision, open to the spirit of creativity. In our formative years, before our minds were conditioned by notions of *professional* and *amateur, creative* and *noncreative,* we reveled in the joys of self-expression, played with imaginary friends, drew pictures of trees, clowns, or rainbows, told stories to ourselves, made clay dinosaurs, drummed and shook tambourines, decorated dollhouses, and went on jungle safaris in the backyard. Should we deny ourselves this magic simply because we are no longer boys and girls?

Self-expression is our birthright, a natural way of reconnecting to the beauty and mystery we experienced as children. To reclaim this birthright, we need only put aside our self-consciousness and immerse ourselves in the creative act, not caring whether we produce work of professional quality. "God is really another artist," said Pablo Picasso. "He invented the giraffe, the elephant and the cat. He has no real style. He just goes on trying other things."

The real goal is to live creatively.

∞ ∞

Try this:

Follow these guidelines when you are practicing an art as a means to inner peace and emotional fulfillment:

1. *Trust yourself.* When engaged in the creative act, honor your intuition. Many of us were never taught to respect our

intuitions, but to believe that if we did what we really wanted
to do, we would fail. Because of this, we often repress our true
inclinations so much that we don't even know what they are.
But by practicing creativity with no goal other than the joy of
self-expression, we can learn to trust ourselves.

2. *Don't censor or criticize yourself.*   Give your imagination
free rein. When you commit yourself to self-expression, you can
create boldly, without caving in to afterthoughts and regret. If
your intuition keeps offering you things and you keep telling it
no, it will stop being so generous. When you accept your ideas
without disparaging them, you will awaken your imagination
and artistic intuition, and open yourself to the unexpected.

3. *Be in the moment.*   Express your authentic feelings. If
you're fearful, express fear. If you're angry, let anger inform your
drawing, your writing, or whatever artistic medium you've
chosen. Honor exactly what's happening inside you when you
take up your paintbrush or bongo drums. Don't try to be other
than what you are. By expressing your feelings at the moment,
you learn self-acceptance. This is another key to using your creative spirit to enhance your inner peace.

4. *Don't analyze.*   This isn't psychotherapy. Express yourself
with no thought of showing people your creations and asking for
feedback or interpretations. Let the practice of whatever art you
have chosen be an end in itself. You can do this by focusing on
the process rather than the end result. Don't think about producing a masterful painting, story, poem, song, or screenplay. Create
for the sheer joy of self-expression. Remember the gratification
you felt as a child while involved in your creativity. This will
help you to break through your conditioning.

5. *Don't worry about talent.*   Who cares whether you have
natural ability or any training? The thought that you should
spend years acquiring technical skills before launching your
own creations will only inhibit your creative spirit.

6. *Practice is an end in itself.*   Express your creative impulses
wholeheartedly. Keep in mind that art is the creative act itself,

and that anything you do with focused consciousness or total awareness is creative. If you look at life this way, you can turn walking, talking, sitting, eating, and breathing into inspiring acts and apply your creative touch to whatever you do.

Revitalizing your creative powers will make you feel young again. No matter how old you are in years, you will be able to cope better with the pressures and craziness of the world. If you develop your self-expression, you will have something beautiful that nobody can take away from you.

Recommended Reading

The Artist's Way: Meeting Your Creative Myths & Monsters by Julia Cameron. Los Angeles: Jeremy P. Tarcher, 1992.
Writing Down the Bones: Freeing the Writer Within by Natalie Goldberg. Boston: Shambhala, 1986.
Writing for Your Life: A Guide and Companion to the Inner Worlds by Deena Metzger. San Francisco: Harper, 1992.
The Zen of Seeing: Seeing/Drawing as Meditation by Frederick Franck. New York: Vintage Books, 1973.

FINDING PEACE THROUGH WORK

Work is love made visible.

—*Kahlil Gibran*

Each of us does some kind of work in this world, but we don't always get paid for it. Whether we make money from it or not, work is one of life's necessities. We must work to live. We work to obtain food, clothing, and shelter; we work to prepare our food; we work to wash our clothing; and we work to keep our shelter clean and in good repair.

All work takes time. It keeps us busy. But is work a drudgery? If it seems so to you, a change of perspective will help.

Try looking at your work in a new way. At its core, work is a way of giving. It is something that we offer of ourselves. We give our work to others and to the world. That's why work can be seen as a way of showing love. As we do our work, whatever it might be —creating, producing, transforming, or solving—we show our love.

In addition, work creates value. It creates value in the world and value within ourselves. Through work, we give something to the world and in turn we are rewarded for it. We create values and get rewards no matter what type of work we do, whether it is work for which we get paid or household chores such as cooking and cleaning.

Obviously, rewards for working are not just financial. Other rewards include:

- a sense of accomplishment
- warm feelings because you're helping others
- pride (Work is a way to offer your unique talents to the world and feel proud of what you do.)
- feeling involved with the world (When you give part of yourself to the world, you make a connection.)
- peace of mind (Satisfaction with your work can bring a feeling of inner calm.)
- happiness (Enjoyment of work leads to happiness in life.)

Simply by working, you can feel fulfilled. Along with numerous emotional rewards, work often brings a tangible reward: money. Don't forget to enjoy and share this, too.

Can work be fun? Yes!

Try this:

1. *Give it your all.*   Whatever work you do, do it to the best of your ability. Furthermore, don't be tempted to degrade your

work, for, as Alexander Chase said, "He who considers his work beneath him will be above doing it well."

2. *Find meaning in what you do.*   Make a list of all the valuable products, ideas, or services you create and all the rewards you gain by working. For this practical exercise, consider all the kinds of work you do, not just the work for which you are paid.

3. *Get involved in your work.*   Whatever you do, do it intensely.

4. *Judge what's fit.*   Remember, there is something heroic in every job that is fit. How do you judge what's fit? If you're taking advantage of people in any way, that type of work is not fit; it may make you money, but you will not feel whole inside or at peace with yourself.

5. *Attend to quality.*   Do your work well: celebrate it. It may even help to forget about tomorrow. "The best preparation for good work tomorrow," said Elbert Hubbard, "is to do good work today."

6. *Do what's needed now.*   In order to help you remain in the moment, stay with each detail of your work until that detail is completed. And remember, details are all there is.

7. *Revere your work.*   Saint Benedict of Nursia said, "To work is to pray." As something that you share with the world, your work is your love. Offer it in that spirit.

CHAPTER 9

Breaking Connections

*B*reaking certain connections in your life will set you free. What are you liberating yourself from? The frenzied pace of the world. Your habits and conditionings. Your negative emotions.

"Wise living," said Eric Hoffer, "consists perhaps less in acquiring good habits than in acquiring as few habits as possible."

Many of our problems result from our emotional conditionings. Confronted with someone or something that gets on our nerves, we may react with anger, fear, disparagement, or hopelessness because it has become our habit to do so. Often these learned behaviors are unthinking, mechanical, and emotionally stultifying. They block us from our genuine, spontaneous responses to the world and the emotional fulfillment that would accompany them.

To unlearn this conditioned behavior and free ourselves of its hypnotic effects, we must understand how other people and the world impact our emotional selves. To succeed, we must be willing to confront our negative emotions without reacting in our usual ways. This process presents us with a challenge, for what we are facing is unpleasant. It might mean relinquishing the overwhelming lure of the media or our own addictive desires, both of which unsettle us and make us slaves to unworthy modes of behavior. But whatever behavior we need to change, we must first see it for what it is, to determine exactly how it affects our lives.

The process of unlearning might involve a temporary withdrawal from the world, until we see clearly the adverse effects it
has on us. Or this process may involve our living in the world as
usual yet employing certain means to break through the conditionings whenever they arise. In either case, we need to focus on
breaking emotional habits that unsettle us and keep us from living
to our utmost potential.

The methods in this chapter are designed to teach you how
to break your emotional habits by transforming their negative
energy into the power of inner peace.

STARTING TO STOP

*All motion in this world has its origin in something that is not
motion.*

—G. C. Lichtenberg

We live our lives in continuous motion. Like waves in the ocean,
we move without interruption from one posture to the next, each
posture flowing into the other without pausing. And we do this day
in, day out, remaining active each day until we fall asleep at night.

Yet what's really happening? Our activity is part of us, but it's
on the periphery. It's on the outside part of us, the part that inter-
acts with the world. It is through our actions that we connect ourselves to the world.

In this sense, our activity takes us from our center—that
is, unless we remain meditative in what we do. Even when the
activity is slight, as with breathing, eye movements (while reading
a book or watching TV), and muscle twitches, it happens apart
from our center.

In meditation, we often focus on breathing because breathing
happens inside of us and helps us get close to our center. But the
activity of breathing is not the center.

Activity implies doing. Activity is motion. At the center,
there is no motion. At the center is being. Activity, even the
activity of thinking or breathing, takes us away from this center.

Our true center, which we can find by meditating, is located some-where behind our breathing and below our thinking.

But the body and the mind have been conditioned to non-stop motion, to go through life in activity, to living at the periphery of ourselves, not the center. When we practice techniques to stop ourselves in our tracks, we glimpse the center.

How does this work? Energy drives all of our motion. Because energy cannot be destroyed, it continues even when we stop our motion. Where does it go? Within. It lights up the center.

George Gurdjieff, who studied many spiritual traditions, became a spiritual leader himself in the 1930s and 1940s. He attracted a broad following of students who used his methods to attain inner peace and a deeper spiritual connection to life. One method Gurdjieff used was a "stop" technique. Occasionally he would yell, "Stop!" and everybody would freeze. If you were talking, you stopped your mouth in whatever sound you were forming. If your eyes were open, you kept them open, not blinking. If you were walking and had one foot off the ground, you kept it off the ground and maintained your pose.

Try it.

When you stop in midactivity like this, something happens. You feel the energy of your action as if the action were continuing. As if witnessing it from a distance, you see the activity for what it really is. Maybe the activity gets you from one place to another. Maybe it helps you to accomplish something. You may see the activity as harmful or you may see it as essential to your survival.

But activity is not all you are. Some part of you is based in nonaction. This is your center, the part of you that you know the least. The center remains peaceful and calm, undisturbed and undisturbable. Just a glimpse of it can instantly bring you peace.

⤳ ⤳

Try this:

Here are two techniques. The first offers a list of ideas to get you started. The second is a specific Tantric sutra that you can use to go to your center.

stop command.   It's helpful when someone else tells
        The command then comes unexpectedly, without
your thinking about telling yourself to stop. Therefore your mind
cannot enter. Indeed, you have no say in the matter. Options for
implementing this technique include:

- Join a Gurdjieff study group, sometimes called Ouspensky/-
  Gurdjieff study group (P. D. Ouspensky helped organize
  Gurdjieff's methods into a system).

- Use the stop command with someone at home—a friend, a
  lover, even a child.

- Use a clock that chimes every fifteen minutes. As soon as you
  hear the tone, stop what you're doing. (Don't watch the clock
  in order to plan your pose. If it doesn't happen spontaneously,
  you'll gain nothing.)

    2. *The Tantric method.*   The sutra is: "Just as you have the
impulse to do something, stop."

    Let's look at a simple impulse first. Say you have an urge to
satisfy your thirst. What do you do? You get a glass, fill it with
water, take it to your lips, and drink. You can tell yourself to stop
anywhere along the way, and ceasing your activity will temporar-
ily halt your impulse to satisfy your thirst.

    Now consider the stop. You can say it silently or you can
say it aloud. But as soon as you say it, stop completely. Don't
blink an eye. Don't breathe. Don't move a muscle. Also, be sure
to stop abruptly. The water in the glass may slosh around from
an abrupt stop, but you will not move. With practice, you can
stop your activity spontaneously anytime. To stop spontaneously: whenever you suddenly feel the urge, stop at once.

    Clearly, each stop ends when you can't hold your breath
any longer. So each may last from twenty seconds to one minute.
When you need to breathe again, do so, and simply resume your
activity as if it had never been interrupted.

    But notice your newfound appreciation for this activity.
Notice what happens. Watch how the stop technique instantly

takes you to your center. Immediately, upon stopping, you can see your activity as if it were a whirlwind swirling around a tranquil and motionless center. Then, when you resume your activity, you'll feel more at one with it, more settled with it, and more calm.

You can use this technique with simple impulses, for instance, when you drop something on the floor, you may have the impulse to pick it up. If so, you can stop yourself anywhere in the motion and realize an instant change in perspective.

In addition, you can use this technique with some powerful impulses, such as the impulse to yell at somebody, the impulse to have sex, or the impulse to take an addictive substance. These impulses are strong. It's hard to stop in the middle of sex. It's hard to halt some anger that causes you to yell. If you're addicted to sugar, drugs, or alcohol, it's hard to say no. But when you do stop such powerful impulses, the energy is magnificent and will take you deep inside yourself. Just be sure that you do not judge the behavior. If you think of an impulse as good or bad, the stop technique will not work. This is because your mind enters. And your mind will consume all the energy when you stop by thinking about how good or bad the impulse was or about how difficult or important it was to stop the impulse.

To use these powerful impulses, consider your anger, sexual desire, or addictive craving as a form of pure energy. In no case is the energy good or bad. What you do with the energy may be good or bad, but the energy itself is neutral. Let it be. Simply watch where it goes when you stop.

Recommended Reading

The Book of Secrets 2 by Bhagwan Shree Rajneesh. San Francisco: Harper Colophon Books, 1979.

Views from the Real World by G. I. Gurdjieff. New York: E.P. Dutton, 1975.

DETACHMENT

By letting go it all gets done
The world is won by those who let it go
But when you try and try
The world is then beyond the swimming.

—*Lao-tzu*

Each of us encounters one major block on the road to inner peace: ego. The ego won't let go. It clings to things. It identifies with objects, possessions, expectations, hopes, dreams, and other tangible and intangible things. In addition, the ego always wants. It wants something more than what it has.

Where do we find ego? It's in our heads. The ego is what we *think* we are. Upon careful inspection, we can see that the ego is a mental construct, a set of preconceived notions we have about ourselves. Yet this construct acts in a powerful manner. It may compel us to fight—not to save our lives but to save our notions, as if attempting to prove, "I'm right and you're wrong."

Known also as our *self*, ego represents our entire identity. How important! Without an identity, we would have no reason to fight. Without a self, why bother? Of course, you would fight if someone attacked you with a knife. But then you would be fighting to save your life, not to prove that your religion is the correct one and therefore entitles you to the holy land, not to prove that you're more worthy or more honorable than your foe, not to prove that your mother doesn't wear combat boots.

Ego wants and ego strives. Ego is achievement oriented. Ego boasts. It brags. Selfishness comes from ego. And unhappiness comes, too, because the ego is never satisfied. There's always something more to want, to gain, or to do.

But look again. In one sense, ego doesn't even exist. Since it is fabricated in the mind and since you can change it by changing your mind, it is an illusion. Yet this illusion affects most of our activity, takes up much of our brain's memory, and blocks us from experiencing reality directly.

Before turning to the methods for releasing your ego, consider this thought from Wu Wei Wu: "Why aren't you happy? It's because ninety-nine percent of everything you do, and think, and say, is for yourself—and there isn't one."

∞ ∞

Try this:

1. *Drop goal-seeking.*   Detach yourself from results. Become thoroughly involved in what you do, but remember that your activity is not you. It's on the periphery. Pay attention to your activity, but forget about its goal. When you do this, each activity can be playful and fun.

Detach yourself even from the results of these exercises. The goal is inner peace, but if you cling to this goal, you will not achieve it. Inner peace will come only when you drop it as a goal. One day you'll be doing something and you'll suddenly realize that you're at peace with yourself.

2. *Let go of personal identities.*   Detach from self. Don't identify with anything. Don't call yourself an alcoholic; don't call yourself a Christian. Why? You can never be utterly one thing. You are always something different, something more.

3. *Not this, not that.*   Notice that whenever a thought comes into your head, you tend to identify with it. You can use a powerful meditation to change this process. When a thought arrives, say, "Not this," or "I am not this." For your next thought, say, "Not that," or "I am not that." For your next thought, say "Not this," and so on. Rather than identifying with your thoughts, you will let them go. Through this method, you can free yourself of mental pressure.

All three methods of bringing about detachment will help you to feel free. By detaching yourself, you release the world. And, in turn, the world releases you.

Detachment is a state of mind. Instead of "I have this" and "I have that," it's "I have nothing." This state of mind is what Seneca was recommending when he said, "We never reflect how pleasant it is to ask for nothing."

DROPPING NEGATIVE DESIRES

How few are our real wants! And how easy is it to satisfy them!
Our imaginary ones are boundless and insatiable.
            —*Julius Charles Hare and Augustus William Hare*

It has been said that human beings are thinking animals. It can as easily be said that human beings are craving animals. That is, we desire innumerable things and experiences that aren't required to sustain our health and survival. A list of these would be endless but would include luxuries and extravagant material objects, excessive food and beverages, illicit drugs, tobacco, success, fame, domination over other people, and numerous sexual experiences. We think we need these things to be happy. Every one of us has at least some of these cravings, and many of us are tormented by them.

If you observe the thoughts that pass through your mind, you'll see that many of them are desires. Because you are interested in achieving peace of mind, some of your desires will be healthy. This is natural, for without desire, how can you realize your potential in life? But you will likely note many desires that are obsessions and cravings for what you don't need. Some may be for things that are detrimental to your health and peace of mind. Perhaps you have cravings that recur and result in substance abuse, overeating, gambling, sexual perversion, or some other unnatural habit that you have adopted over the years. Although not cravings, other negative thoughts function in the same manner, haunting you, plaguing you, pulling you down. For instance, you might find yourself entertaining self-deprecating thoughts, or thinking that your life is a worthless affair.

If you examine your thoughts honestly, you will see that many of them are desires for things you don't need and that these desires, or cravings, come and go with a will of their own. It's not as if you're trying to think them; they pop up in your mind, regardless of any conscious volition to stop them.

Why do we desire things we don't really need? Why do we crave experiences that only deplete our health and sense of well-being? The answer is simple. We believe that the objects of our desire will make us happy.

Yet when we satisfy our cravings, we may eliminate some-thing, such as a half gallon of ice cream or a pint of scotch at one sitting, but we don't eliminate the cravings themselves. They return, often with greater power than before, making a home in our brains and demanding the right to tell us what to do. Cravings are convincing. Even when we recognize the vicious cycle they pro-mote, we often give in to one craving to escape another, hoping the substitution will make us feel better. Trying to satisfy these incessant cravings, we suffer much, waste time and energy, and get nowhere.

Thoreau once said: "A man is rich in proportion of the number of things he can afford to let alone." He wisely understood the relentless nature of desire as well as the secret of happiness, for by *rich* he meant happy or at peace with yourself.

We cannot find happiness and peace of mind by satisfying cravings. We can only be happy through desiring and doing what-ever will bring us greater physical, mental, and spiritual health.

When you realize this, your priorities shift and you begin to entertain the thoughts that create healthy desires. To want a healthy life-style is a positive desire that, if acted upon, will release you from many of your cravings. In the meantime, whenever you feel afflicted by unnatural desires, you can use the following tech-nique to calm yourself.

∞ ∞

Try this:

The next time a craving arises, stop what you're doing and enter-tain this craving. *Entertain* is the key word here. Dwell on the craving, invite it into your mind, don't resist it. Let the desire to satisfy the craving emerge completely in your consciousness, so that you are aware of it dominating all your thoughts. Don't judge or suppress it; give it free rein.

you feel the intensity of the craving, picture yourself
t. If the craving is to drink excessively, see yourself
going to the package store or bar; buying the beer, wine, bourbon, or gin; and drinking it as you would if you yielded to this
craving. Conjure the taste of the drink and the first wave of
intoxication. Mentally drink as many drinks as you would if
physically satisfying the craving. Try to feel the way this much
alcohol usually makes you feel; then summon the feeling you
would have in the morning when you woke up. Entertain these
thoughts as though they were guests—and then drop them, let
them go, and proceed with what you really want to do instead
of drinking.

Strange as it sounds, if you persist with this method, you
will find that you can forget your cravings more easily, because
you neither suppressed them nor gave in to them. You allowed
them to speak, to rage through your brain; you gave them the
space to voice themselves, and you felt the intensity of their
energy, without trying to diminish or control it.

After trying this technique, take stock of your energy level
and state of mind. Do you feel renewed? Do you feel stronger or
more calm?

From time to time you may give in to cravings. If you keep
trying, however, you'll find that by entertaining them fully and
then dropping them, you will convert their negative, obsessive
power into a creative energy that revitalizes you and leaves you
feeling more at peace with yourself.

When this happens, use this renewed power to fulfill your
desires for a healthier and more serene life-style. And whatever
happens along the way, remember that reality doesn't exist to
meet your expectations. This thought, together with the practice
of dropping negative desires, will help you immensely as you
aspire to a life of inner peace.

Recommended Reading

Scientific Healing Affirmations by Paramahansa Yogananda. Los
Angeles: Self-Realization Fellowship, 1985.

DROPPING INTO SILENCE

Speech is of time, silence is of eternity.

—*Thomas Carlyle*

In the Himalaya Mountains, you can find many places where there is silence. In these places, you may find someone sitting quietly with half-open eyes, and when you get closer, you'll distinguish a slight smile upon the person's face.

People seeking inner peace often seek places of silence. That's why monasteries are built on secluded mountaintops. On an undeveloped mountain, you are removed from the noise of the marketplace, the town, or the city. You are free of all the hustle and bustle.

There is peace in silence. When you sit noiselessly in a quiet place, your perspective changes. Try it. No doubt, the deepest peace on earth exists in the utter stillness of the mind. At first, to experience this stillness, it will help if you practice in a quiet environment. A silent place can help to clear your mind. With no distractions outside of you, you need only contend with your inner distractions—your thoughts, the noise of your mind. And soon, they too will quiet down.

We talk so much, often needlessly. If nobody talked unless he or she had something worth saying, the noise level on this planet would diminish considerably. As Lewis Carroll wrote of Alice in his *Diary on "Alice"*, "It was more that she had to say something, than that she had something to say."

So let's learn to be quiet together, even though it is difficult. "We are used to the actions of human beings," said V. S. Pritchett, "not to their stillness." It's time we started getting used to the stillness. We can practice silence within ourselves and appreciate it more within others.

☞ ☞

Here's how:

1. *Be silent in a silent place.* Have you ever felt the need to retreat to a silent place? Well, stop thinking about it and do it. Choose a silent place where you can stay. Options include

mountains, forests, and national parks, or go to a yoga ashram that offers a silent retreat program.

Plan the trip for yourself, and don't be afraid to be alone. In order to achieve deep silence, you almost always have to be alone. Don't be concerned if at first you feel uncomfortable when you're alone and silent. You're just not used to it. Your silence will soon set you free and bring you a feeling of inner peace.

Plan to do this for two days every three months. Or plan a one- or two-week trip once a year. Or do both.

2. *Be silent in the everyday world.* Too much noise interferes with inner peace. So take as many breaks from your noisy world as possible. How?

First, schedule times of silence each day—fifteen minutes here, fifteen minutes there. At work, when you take a break, move as far from the noise as possible. Remain by yourself for the moments and simply enjoy the peace and quiet. At home, if your family will cooperate, you can take some time to be silent. Your family members may even want to participate together in a few moments of calm; if not, try scheduling your time at home when everyone is out or asleep. It is said that the quietest time of the day is 4 to 5 A.M. This is a great time to sit quietly or take a solitary walk.

Second, drive in silence. Turn off your radio, tape deck, or compact disc player. Listen to the sounds around you. Let yourself become one with the sounds, even if you're on a busy freeway. You'll be astounded at the difference this can make. It transforms drive time into calm time.

Third, have a meal in silence with a loved one. Or simply sit and gaze into one another's eyes. Communing in silence with another person creates some of the most beautiful and compelling feelings we can experience.

Fourth, stop talking for one whole day. Take a few days each year during which you do not talk at all. You'll find this technique difficult because most people around you will not want to cooperate. But it's powerful and worth doing. When you spend a day in silence, you will understand that language itself is

relatively meaningless, that people talk mainly to fill gaps in
time, and that something deeper than words is much more
important to human beings.

Fifth, let more things rest in silence. Often you can say
more with silence than you can with words. Why fill the air with
idle chatter? Indeed, as Pindar said in his *Odes*, "Many a time the
thing left silent makes for happiness."

Recommended Reading:

Choose to Live Peacefully by Susan Smith Jones, Ph.D. Berkeley, CA:
Celestial Arts, 1991.

LETTING YOURSELF GO CRAZY

*See, the human mind is kind of like . . . a pinata. When it breaks
open, there's a lot of surprises inside. Once you get the pinata
perspective, you see that losing your mind can be a peak experience.*
— *Jane Wagner*

The modern world can madden us. Each day we are subjected to a
barrage of signals, noise, and information. We can't escape the sensory bombardment of advertising and the mass media. It's enough
to make anyone crazy. That most of our hospitals and jails are overcrowded is but one indication of our inability to cope with the
stresses of the modern world.

We live in a society where something changes every day as
we reach new levels of mind-boggling technology. In a world of
"virtual reality," genetic engineering, biocide, ozone depletion,
subliminal advertising, genocide, serial killers, hot and cold wars,
deforestation, and the ever-present threat of nuclear holocaust,
how can we possibly ingest and assimilate all that is happening?

We can't.

It's impossible to process the awesome changes and unpre-
dictable events of each day without going bonkers. But, unless
we become hermits, we can't ignore what is happening because it

is broadcast to us from all sides. To live in society, we must expect to put up with innumerable stresses, strains, and unforeseeable changes.

What can you do about it? How can you keep your peace of mind in the midst of this madness and chaos? Let yourself go crazy. This isn't a joke. In our world, everyone deserves to go consciously crazy at least once a day.

∽   ∽

Try this:

The situation is that you've heard and seen all you can stand. You've had it. You feel outraged, paranoid, destructive. You want to throw your dinner plates against the wall or put your fist through it. You want to have a stiff shot of bourbon or scream at someone.

Stop. Don't do any of these things. Save your china for your next dinner party. Don't rush out and buy a gun. Don't smash your neighbor's picture window. Don't put your fist through the wall. Save yourself the legal and medical expenses.

Go to your bedroom. Lock the door. Take off your clothes. Look at yourself in the mirror. (If you don't have a mirror in your bedroom, get one. In the meantime, use your bathroom.) See all the craziness of the world straining behind your twitching eyes, clamped teeth, tight muscles, and the heave of your pent-up chest.

Now cut loose. Explode with everything you have. Scream, shriek, moan, cry, cackle, and laugh diabolically. Express yourself and every little or big madness you've been forced to swallow like poison on this typical day of modern times. Jump, shake, make faces, dance, throw punches, froth, babble, stamp, stab your imaginary knife, fire your invisible gun. Go completely nuts, and don't worry about losing your mind. You will keep it, rest assured. In fact, this investment in conscious craziness will bring you greater peace and sanity.

When you have let yourself go mad in front of the mirror for a good ten minutes, fall down as though dead. Lie on the floor until you feel like getting back up and wondering what you want for dinner.

By the way, if you share your home with a roommate, spouse, or lover and you don't want him or her to call 911, follow the above instructions closely, making as little external noise as possible. Prolong and savor your silent screams.

Recommended Reading:

Crazy Wisdom by Wes "Scoop" Nisker. Berkeley, California: Ten Speed Press, 1990.

JUST SAY NO TO THE MEDIA

> *All media exist to invest our lives with artificial perceptions and arbitrary values.*
>
> —*Marshall McLuhan*

We are surrounded by media. In fact, forms of media so pervade our world we can surely consider them a major portion of the environment. Televisions, newspapers, billboards, movies, books, radios, and magazines are everywhere.

It's big business, for along with imparting information, the media must sell sponsors' products in order to survive. Advertising copy and TV commercials are designed to catch immediate attention and persuade us to buy products which we are either subtly or blatantly told we need in order to be popular, accepted, lovable, successful, satisfied, secure, and happy. The psychological lure is there; we hear it and see it whenever we turn on the tube or open a magazine. In these colorful ads, stunningly handsome and excitingly beautiful models pose as perfectly successful men and women who are perfectly successful because they use the right deodorant, drive the right car, or drink the right scotch. Sex appeal is equated with success and we, the consumers, must use the latest products and dress in the latest fashions or else live lonely, antiquated lives.

Also with this message, we are told we must stay informed, as if it is a moral imperative. If you don't read the newspaper or watch the six o'clock news, how can you expect to be a responsible citizen? If you aren't up on the current trends, how can you expect to be a success? These are the unspoken messages that accompany our information-delivering environment; this is the media's sales pitch.

Sex and fear are the basic motivators used by magazines and television and radio stations to sell products. It seems as though both sex and fear, usually in the form of violence, are presented more graphically every year. Marshall McLuhan called television a "cool medium" because it involves two of your senses. Its quick cuts, flashing images of lust, and screams of brutality leave us staring at the screen, mesmerized and desensitized. The engineered presentation of the news is especially numbing. There is a reason for this, according to media psychologists. The images advance too rapidly for the conscious mind to assimilate even a fraction of their sensational content. This process stupefies the conscious mind and hypnotizes the viewer. In this trancelike state, viewers are vulnerable to advertising, which is most effective when it appeals directly to our unconscious minds. When the commercial comes on, we are impressionable subjects, easily seduced by the sponsor's message: Buy our product!

Craving Information

An addiction is something to which you devote yourself habitually or compulsively until a part of you thinks it needs this thing on a regular basis. In a world where the media pervade and persuade, we need to keep up with the latest fashions, news, and mad flurry of information that is hurled at us pell-mell. But we don't need these things the way we need food, shelter, water, and other basic goods. This doesn't mean that you shouldn't keep abreast of current events or that you should dress yourself in the clothes your grandparent wore. But take a minute to examine your motives for watching television, reading magazines and newspapers, and listening to the radio, as well as for buying the products which these media endorse.

You know the expression, "You are what you eat." It can be readily applied to our information-glutted environment. Information is a food—a food for the mind. If you find yourself craving it excessively, ask yourself why. Is your life so boring that you can't do without these hits of sensationalism each day? More importantly, how do you feel after watching television for long hours or reading the morning and evening editions of the paper every day? Do these activities lift your spirits or elate you? The following suggestions will help you answer these questions.

⌒ ⌒

Try this:

1. *Take a break.*   For one evening each week, don't watch TV. Instead, watch your breath or practice one of the other methods in this book, a method you can do at home. Then take stock of yourself; see how you feel. Do you believe you have missed anything by not watching TV this evening? Do you feel more calm, rested, or energetic?

You can apply this practice to other media or stretch the evening into an entire day in which you don't read newspapers and magazines, nor turn on the radio or TV. This "media fast," if done on a regular basis, especially when you feel mentally overloaded, can be most beneficial for breaking cultural conditioning and media addiction, which mostly leave us depressed, stuporous, or emotionally upset.

2. *Watch carefully.*   Try watching the six o'clock news with the sound turned off. This experience can give you insight into exactly how this medium is used. See how many of the broadcast images involve sex or violence. Notice the newscasters' faces as they report crimes, especially murder or other atrocities. Are their expressions appropriate to the content of the information? Count the number of images that are presented to you in a half hour. How are the commercials presented?

3. *Consider what you need to know.*   What good does it do to get worked up over all the wars and barbaric acts that are reported to you from around the globe each day? Is it a service to yourself or others to become depressed over "the state of the world"?

The best way to promote peace in the world is to promote peace within yourself first; without it, your efforts will only create more unrest. Realizing this, you will know that inner peace begins with being responsible to yourself.

These experiments can help you determine your relationship to the media, understand how it affects you, and decide whether you are a media addict. They can also help you to break your addiction.

Choosing a healthy mental diet is as important to your well-being and peace of mind as choosing a healthy physical diet of food and exercise.

Recommended Reading

Media Sexploitation by Wilson Bryan Key. New York: Signet, 1976.
News from Nowhere by Edward Jay Epstein. New York: Vintage
       Books, 1974.
Watching Television edited by Todd Gitlin. New York: Pantheon
       Books, 1986.

BREAKING YOUR CULTURAL CONDITIONING

*It can't be mere coincidence that random violence is increasing at
the same time that such violence is mythologized in mass culture;
that out-of-wedlock childbirth is increasing at the same time that
unfettered sexual indulgence is celebrated in the same culture; that
respect for education and self-discipline is declining at the same time
that the culture places a higher value on inarticulate self-expression
and unlimited self-gratification.*

                                                    —*Jonathan Yardley*

Culture is traditionally represented in the art, the music, and the writings of a people. Through these representations, people pass on the images they have of themselves. Today's main conduit for culture in the United States is the media. Through a given medium, certain individuals transmit ideas and images to other individuals in our culture. The primary media of modern times include TV, radio, films, books, magazines, and newspapers.

So how do we Americans see ourselves? Let's take a look.

All too often, our cultural outlets paint us as a savage and murderous lot with abundant and irrepressible cravings for sex. Violence and sex. How much can we take?

First consider the presentation of violence in the media. Everyone in this society sees too much violence, and it affects us all profoundly. A recent study estimated that, by the age of eighteen, children living in homes with cable TV are exposed to 30,000 violent deaths and another 40,000 violent acts (in which the victims don't die).

In addition, the movies are rife with brutality. Cinematic violence has become more graphic, more horrifying, more sadistic, and more common in recent years than at any other time in the history of film.

What about our music? For the first time in the history of music, songs produced for the mass culture have depicted all manner of violence. These songs, released during the past ten to fifteen years, have glorified rape, murder, fighting, even "cop killing."

And in a recent study of best-selling books, the National Conference on Television Violence found a 61 percent increase in antisocial or proviolence themes in fiction from 1966 to 1988. What's worse, the violent themes have become more gruesome. For example, satanic and horror themes are now common among bestsellers yet were nonexistent before the 1960s.

So much for violence. What about sex? If you're titillated regularly by sexual images, can it frustrate your natural sex drive?

For all of history until the 1900s, when humans were titillated sexually, it was almost always by a real person, not the image of a person. And it almost always led to a consummated sexual act. Now we may be sexually aroused hundreds of times in any given week, but only a few of these times are consummated in sex. Furthermore, most of the sexual titillations come from images of people rather than real people. These images entice us from larger-than-life billboards, expose themselves in our living rooms in brilliant patterns on smaller-than-life TV screens, tantalize us from the pages of newspapers and magazines (usually in the form of stunning advertisements), or reach with long arms out of movie screens to tickle us with erotic pleasure. And that's not all, for we can actually gorge ourselves on more explicit material if we're willing to spend a few dollars and seek out sources such as pornographic movies and magazines, not to mention phone-sex lines.

The message about sex from the media seems to be: "Get it on. Do it. Don't stop. Let it grip you." Especially, "Let it grip you," because the more it grips you, the more the media can influence you with it. Obviously, the media uses sex to compel you to watch a particular show, read a particular magazine, go to a particular movie, buy a particular product, and so on.

But ultimately, how satisfying is it to view so much sex? How satisfying is it to view violence?

Consider these lines from a 1993 column by David Broder: "Since 1960, there has been a 560 percent increase in violent crime, more than a 400 percent increase in illegitimate births, a quadrupling of divorce rates, a tripling of the percentage of children living in single parent homes, more than a 200 percent increase in the teenage suicide rate, a drop of almost 80 points in the SAT (pre-college scholastic aptitude test) scores."

And consider this information from a 1992 article by Dr. Lee Salk:

The Top Seven School Problems in the 1940s

1. talking in class
2. chewing gum
3. making noise

4. running in the halls
5. cutting in line
6. dress code violations
7. littering

The Top Seven School Problems in the 1990s

1. drug abuse
2. alcohol abuse
3. pregnancy
4. suicide
5. rape
6. robbery
7. assault

Now take a look inside yourself. Would you consciously do something that increases your tension or makes you feel unhappy? You probably wouldn't. But you do just that each time you watch violence on TV, read about a murder in the newspaper, read a satanic-cult novel, see a gory movie, or listen to a song describing rape. You will also feel unhappy and tense with any media-generated sexual stimulation because it only serves to frustrate you. It keeps you wanting but never getting.

Think about violence for a minute. What do you gain by witnessing brutal acts? Does it meet some crucial inner need? Or is the media preying on your natural fears? Whether the media is reporting real-life violence in the form of "news" or prefabricating the violence as part of a story, you gain nothing but anguish.

Watching violence makes you feel fearful inside, and fear is a strong emotion. It compels you. It gives you a rush. And this is the problem. You can become addicted to the rush. So the media has you trapped. How do you get out of the trap? Stop viewing, listening to, or reading media presentations of violence.

Now think for a minute about sex in the media. What does it add to your life? It feels stimulating, even exhilarating, and unlike

violence, which leaves you with a grimace, sexual images leave you
with a smile. But it's an anxious smile, an incomplete smile, a leering
smile, because these portrayals increase your desire without satisfying it. Thus sex in the media puts you in a state of unrest. That's
the point. Sex probably causes fewer problems than violence, but
if it leaves you unsettled, what good is it?

Sex can bring positive feelings of wonder, but its beauty is
ultimately diminished by an excess of synthetic images. Sex in the
media exists to lure you into buying a product or watching a show.

ᝐ ᝐ

Try this:

1. *Take these tests.*

Media Test #1 (violence)

In the past week:

How many violent crimes did you see on TV shows or in the movies,
read about in newspapers, magazines, or books, and hear about on the radio
(in speech or in a song)? Add up the numbers: _____

Count how many violent crimes you actually witnessed in real life: _____

Now ask yourself how closely what you see and hear in the media matches
your real life: _____

_____

Yet how much does the media affect you? Consider these
questions:

		Yes	No
1.	*When TV shows, newspapers, movies, books, magazines, or songs present you with violent crimes, does it improve your health in any way?*	☐	☐
2.	*Does it improve your outlook on the world?*	☐	☐
3.	*Does it make you more peaceful?*	☐	☐
4.	*Does it make you more fun-loving?*	☐	☐
5.	*Does it make you more fearful?*	☐	☐

	Yes	No
6. *Does it sometimes leave you disgusted?*	☐	☐
7. *Does it ever cause nightmares?*	☐	☐
8. *Does it cause you to feel nervous about crime, perhaps producing a feeling that a crime is very likely to happen to you?*	☐	☐

Media Test #2 (sex)

In the past week:

How many sexually titillating images did you see on TV, at the movies, on billboards, or in magazines, books, and newspapers and how many did you hear about (in an arousing way) on the radio, in a song, or by calling a phone sex line? Add up the numbers: _____

Count how many times you were sexually titillated in real life (this could be a high number if you spent the week at the beach): _____

Here's the important part: How many times did you follow through on the titillation? (In other words, after the titillation began, how many times did you enter into a sexual act that ended in orgasm?) _____

How many of these times were you with another person? _____

How many times were you alone? _____

Consider the number of times you engaged in sex compared to the number of times you were titillated by images and answer these questions:

	Yes	No
1. *Does the media seem to overstimulate you sexually?*	☐	☐
2. *Do you think the media attempts to manipulate you with sexual images?*	☐	☐
3. *Does the media's constant output of sexual images ever cause you to feel uncomfortable about your own sexual image?*	☐	☐
4. *Do the images you see in the media ever make you want a partner who looks different (for instance, more like the model in an advertisement or like the* Playgirl *or* Playboy *centerfold)?*	☐	☐
5. *Do sexual images in the media help you to feel more peaceful?*	☐	☐

2. *Avoid the media.*   If any part of you feels less peaceful because of the media, start to shun these systems of mass communication. Why bother with them? Take a step in the opposite
direction.

If you want to avoid the media selectively, do so. For
instance, if violence is the main problem, stop watching violent
movies and TV shows, including TV news. Also avoid the newspaper (except perhaps for the sports and entertainment sections).
And don't tempt yourself by saying that you're strong enough to
handle just one more violent show. You don't need to prove anything.

In addition, be prepared. Whenever an image that you
don't like appears, change the channel, turn the page, stop
reading the article, or turn your head. Push it away. Look at the
situation this way: it's as if you had just quit smoking yet
someone was constantly there lighting a cigarette for you and
trying to put it in between your lips. Be prepared to push it away.

Make a firm commitment to eschew media violence or
media sex or both. Make it a vow to yourself. Now, to help you
keep this vow, write down the benefits of continuing to avoid
violence or sex transmitted by the media. Do this once a month.
You'll find that you gain such benefits as "a greater sense of secu-
rity," "having fewer fears," "an improved sensuality," and even
"deeper feelings of love for others."

CHAPTER 10

Humor

*W*hy do we find the fool, the jester, and the clown so lovable? It's because they are not preoccupied with their own importance, because they are willing to laugh at themselves, and more than anything, because they reveal the absurdities of human behavior.

In a seesaw world overly weighted with seriousness, the fool jumps up and down on the lighter end of the plank, trying his damnedest to overthrow the force of gravity. That he never succeeds doesn't concern him; his only concern is the passion he puts into his effort. It is this passion that we love, secretly if not openly. It is the fool's fervent antics to beat all odds that win us over.

The fool's topsy-turvy world exists within each of us, awaiting discovery. It is up to us to find and claim it, and to bring its much-needed dimension into our lives.

Mirth is so enjoyable it dispels our solemnity and tension in an instant. No other stress-reliever is as quick and as sure as laughter, or as much fun. A sense of humor is the best antidote for all the depressing thoughts we have upon reading the day's headlines or watching the six o'clock news. This doesn't mean that we make light of the horrors of the world, but that we need not let them get us down.

Laughter is a corrective we can use to remain balanced in a chaotic world. Regarding our need to laugh, the great circus clown

Grock had this to say: "I am not at all the kind of man who wants to make merry only in the circus, and for the rest of his time goes about like any ordinary citizen, solid and self-contained. My attitude has always been that if I am a clown in the ring I can and should be a clown out of the ring. Either you should be a thing or not be it."

Humor puts problems in perspective. It is liberating to laugh, especially at ourselves. Think of what sometimes happens when you're having a bad day: Everything that could go wrong has gone wrong, and you become wrapped up in anger, frustration, and self-pity. Things get worse and worse until you reach a critical point — when you are cooking your dinner and manage to spill the soup pot. Now the absurdity of your bad day is such that you can do nothing but laugh before cleaning up the mess. At that moment of laughter, you conquer your bad mood and enjoy the cosmic joke that has been played on you.

When you practice methods for achieving inner peace, you will most likely experience sudden shifts in perspective about yourself and the world. Many of these shifts will make you want to laugh. When this happens, seize the opportunity. Such laughter brings insight and healing and can put you at one with the universe. You can go even further from there by following Woody Allen's advice: "Students achieving oneness will move ahead to twoness."

ARE YOU MISSING THE GREATEST COMEDY IN LIFE?

The most wasted day is that in which we have not laughed.
—Nicolas Chamfort

Many writers have acknowledged that man is a laughing animal. Our species' unique ability to laugh provides us with a great deal of enjoyment in life. Through laughter, we free ourselves of the many cares and worries we face during our brief sojourns on this earth. The French writer Rabelais, who embodied the comedic spirit in his work, said, "For all your ills I give you laughter."

Laughter raises us from the gloomy depths of our one-track minds and makes us see what fools we are to remain somber so much of the time. If a fifteenth-century court jester were expressing this thought, he might say, "Laughing is the only thing you shouldn't take lightly."

To be sure, laughter is one of life's greatest pleasures. Those endowed with a rich sense of humor can view life as a comedy. Such people certainly live more zestful lives than those who see only tragedy.

In today's world of sense-slamming spectacles, the need to free ourselves from our wound-up minds is greater than ever. For starters, we can go to a hilarious movie or visit a comedy club for an evening of cathartic release. Yet much of our sense of humor remains untapped when we only seek its sources outside ourselves. We can develop a much greater sense of humor if we change our perspective by ceasing to take life so seriously.

If our cats and dogs and canaries and hamsters could speak, they would probably tell us that human life is truly a comedy of errors. And this is how it should be, for it is through our willingness to make mistakes and our self-effacement after having done so, that we human beings remain open-minded. With our readiness to accept life for what it is and our courage to consider what it could have been, the proverbial banana peel under our feet and the custard pie in our face become sources of levity.

That we will be slipping on banana peels and wiping custard from our cheeks for the rest of our days is a given, accepted by those of us with the ability to laugh at ourselves. If you miss the opportunity to laugh at yourself, you are missing life's greatest comedy. When you find humor in your own shortcomings, troubles, or bad luck, you at once relax and become more tolerant of the human condition. You feel more of a player and less of a victim on the stage of life. Then the traffic jams, burnt toast, leaky toilets, stubbed toes, and other minor daily catastrophes can remind you that it is time to have a good laugh.

Life doesn't exist to meet our expectations. So why get worked up over those pies and banana peels? Why not accept them as inevitable and make light of our own foolish demands that this slippery, stubborn jackass of a world hold still while we saddle it with our dreams and desires? This is the rut of seriousness and self-importance. If we get stuck in it, we lose our humor—that wonderful sense with which we were born. Bitching and moaning over unexpected traffic jams or rainy days when we had planned a picnic only make matters worse. The attitude that little difficulties are not worth getting upset over can keep us on an even keel and save us untold aggravation; but the capacity to laugh at life's inconveniences can turn negativity into a healthy, vital energy.

It is a medically proven fact that laughter has a healing quality. Laughter can slow down heart rates and reduce blood pressure. Its healing effects are evident in the real-life account of the writer Norman Cousins, who, when faced with a diagnosed incurable illness, shut himself in a room and spent his time in bed, watching the movies of Laurel and Hardy, Charlie Chaplin, and Buster Keaton on videotape and reading through a stack of comic novels. Having made this conscious decision to laugh several years ago, Norman Cousins is still with us today, actively writing and living with a redeemed sense of life and laughter.

If you can promote the miracle of healing by indulging in comedy, consider the value of laughter as a preventive health measure. And it's such a pleasurable one to practice! You don't have to join a fitness club or buy any special paraphernalia. You can enjoy a good laugh alone or with others and find a wealth of moments in the day to laugh.

Here's how:

There is a method to this madness. If you have trouble laughing, let your body do the groundwork. Tomorrow, when you wake up in bed, contract your stomach muscles, open your mouth, and laugh. Contract your stomach muscles, roll your belly, and simulate a laugh. Do this for a good five minutes. This exercise will firm up your waistline, loosen your diaphragm (a big tension spot in the body), and leave you breathing freely all morning. A few days of feigned laughter may be necessary to set off the real thing. But soon, as you listen to yourself doing this absurd experiment, your mock laugh will become a real one. The more ridiculous you let yourself be, the more you can howl and roll your belly, the greater your chances for exploding in laughter.

This is an easy exercise to undertake if you sleep alone. But if you have a spouse or lover who is too glum and sluggish to join in your wake-up shenanigans, get up, go to the bathroom, shut the door, and make faces in the mirror—one after another, the most foolish, embarrassing faces you can think of. Simulate the face of happiness, silliness, goofiness, the face of the baboon, the lion, the snake, the sad-eyed dog. Watching yourself making these faces will fill you with a glorious chaos of emotions. After all, this is what most of us did as kids. Don't be afraid of being silly or ridiculous. After a few days, you won't be able to help laughing at yourself, laughing with yourself, laughing without rhyme or reason.

Once you allow yourself this fun, you will feel saner and more calm. This five-minute surrender to zaniness each morning will cue you in to all the opportunities for laughter during your day. Soon you will see yourself in a new light, like a clown at the circus, and begin to laugh at yourself in the car, the office, waiting in line at the store, or stalking down the street to an appointment or meeting. Anytime you catch yourself going about with a grim face, stop and laugh your wrought-up tension away. If you make laughter a personal habit, you will save yourself from a world of stress. And when you tell a joke, laugh at it yourself. Who said we shouldn't laugh at our own jokes? That notion only makes you miss out on half the fun of telling them.

In addition, you can watch funny movies, as Norman Cousins did, or go to comedy clubs. Also, many holistic health centers and retreats, such as the Omega Institute in Rhinebeck, New York, offer programs designed to develop your sense of humor.

Laughter is a healthy habit, and no other habit offers so much fun. Laugh every chance you get, and enjoy the greatest comedy in life.

Recommended Reading:

The Search for Signs of Intelligent Life in the Universe by Jane Wagner. New York: Harper & Row, 1986.

SMILING

We have no more right to consume happiness without producing it than to consume wealth without producing it.

—*George Bernard Shaw*

The half smile of the Buddha reveals the depth of his inner peace. You can see this on most statues and carvings that depict this world teacher. His half smile symbolizes the cheerful serenity that is latent in all of us.

In the Buddha's Eastern homeland, there evolved a system of bodily expressions called *mudras*, in which different gestures create different emotional states. The beauty of this system lies in the use of the body's expressiveness to feel more at one with yourself. If, for instance, you bring your palms together by your chest and bow your head slightly, you will likely feel reverent and prayerful as you maintain this gesture. The native Americans prayed, communed with nature, and expressed their reverence for life by standing with their arms raised to the sky, as though receiving grace through their open hands. This gesture enabled the first Americans to assume the state of mind needed to practice their spirituality.

From this perspective, smiling itself is a *mudra*—and a powerful one. When you're joyful and feel a sense of well-being, you smile. In the same manner, when you are calm you express the calmness in your breathing, which becomes slow and regular. In each case, your expressiveness starts in the mind and moves through the body. As breathing calmly can relax your mind, smiling can make you feel happier.

Try this:

When you wake up in the morning and go into the bathroom, look at yourself in the mirror and smile. Tell yourself you feel good about being alive, thankful for your life. Feel the goodness of this expression and how it cheers you. Tell yourself you will remember to smile throughout the day.

Smile in the company of others whenever it's appropriate. At these moments, feel the expressiveness of your smile. Allow your good nature to radiate from your face.

This simple practice will make you feel good about yourself and help others to feel relaxed and comfortable in your presence.

Recommended Reading

The Miracle of Mindfulness: A Manual on Meditation by Thich Nhat Hanh. Boston: Beacon Press, 1975.

CHAPTER 11

Love

*L*ove makes connections and breaks connections at the same time. You have to give love in order to keep it. You can't possess the object of your love and expect to experience love. If you do, then the thought that you are a loving person is a delusion.

To love, you must be vulnerable. You need to put aside all your expectations and all your thoughts of possession or self-gratification. Your mind must be clear and your heart open. Then you can give of yourself to others with no thoughts of return.

The thought of such openness might be scary if you have been emotionally wounded repeatedly. You might even have turned love into a strategy to appease your own desires. But, in the end, this never works.

Our world contains so much suffering, unrest, and despair partly because we've invested in the strategy of giving love only when we think we can get something in return, mistaking this arrangement for genuine love. In reality, this strategy allows us to hide from our emotional wounds. And how can we love when we are wounded?

To love, we must be healthy and whole. Love begins as a healing and loving of ourselves. This self-love is not selfishness but the prerequisite to loving others. As we open our armored hearts and allow love to enter, we heal our emotional selves. Only when we feel good about ourselves and rejoice in our own lives can we give ourselves to others with no expectations.

The great American poet Walt Whitman implied this when he said: "Dazzling and tremendous how quick the sun-rise would kill me, / If I could not now and always send sun-rise out of me."

How fast and deeply we wound ourselves when the sun of our supposed love leaves us in the dark! Yet real love is not circumstantial. It doesn't depend on a condition outside of ourselves that, when it isn't met, leaves us feeling hateful, anxious, and depressed. Rather, love is an overflowing of the energy that comes from our loving ourselves.

In this chapter, you will learn how to heal your emotional wounds and open your heart. In addition, you will discover ways to drop all thoughts of yourself and the other, and to become the act of loving.

OPENING THE HEART

When one loves somebody, everything is clear—where to go, what to do—it all takes care of itself and one doesn't have to ask anybody about anything.

—*Maksim Gorky*

Have you ever loved somebody—truly loved somebody? True love doesn't want to possess the beloved. It wants to set him or her free. Moreover, true love sets the lover free as well.

Indeed, love frees us from ourselves, from the gripping weight of our egos. The ego is a false self, a self created by the mind and separate from the body. The ego is never satisfied. It always wants this, that, and more; and when some desire is filled, the ego goes on wanting.

On the other hand, love is satisfaction itself, mainly because love dissolves the ego. Ego separates us from others. Love connects us. Ego divides us from within. Love fulfills us. Ego creates conflict. Love creates peace.

Also, true love is giving. At its core, love means giving up the self. It is surrender. As you release your self, you sink into a deeper being within, a being that radiates love. The moment you form any idea of getting something in return for love, as soon as you want to possess, you lose it. When you love, you don't want. You offer something. You create something for someone else. So remember this: whenever you say, "I want," you stop loving.

Love creates a connection. That's why thoughts of self can get in the way. The self shows us how we're different; love shows us how we're the same. All major spiritual traditions affirm that true love is selfless.

Our love connects us to others and connects us to the world. The Bible offers many definitions of God: God is "the creator," God is "the father," and so on. In the New Testament, one definition occurs most often: "God is love." There's a good reason. Love opens the heart. Love invites connection. You will discover no more accessible human emotion to connect you to God than love. Through love, you will realize the God within you.

Therefore be aware of two truths as you go through life. Whenever you're loving, you'll find you're at one with God. And whenever you're loving, you'll find you're at peace with the world.

It will help to know one more thing. Scientists have proven that loving feelings generate peacefulness. When experiencing love, your body produces endorphins (morphine-like biochemicals) that leave you feeling peaceful and calm.

∽ ∽

Try this:

When you feel love, become the loving. Pay no attention to the person you are. Forget about being a lover, forget about the beloved. Involve yourself totally in the loving energy and let it pour out of you.

This is easier when you don't try to express love in words. Instead, radiate love with your body. Pay attention to your heart; imagine your heart showing love. The throbbing we feel in love is the throbbing of the heart.

Secondly, show love in sex. Through its strong, energetic connection with another human being, sex shakes you with the energy of love. That's why, during sex, if you release the mind, it's easy to open the heart. So whenever you engage in sex, allow this opening. Allow love to enter. (To help with this, see chapter 13.)

Finally, remember to show love as an integral part of your life. Reveal your love to others every chance you get. Live love. Let love be your attitude toward life. If you make love your top priority, you will live a joyous life.

ALLOWING LOVE TO ENTER

To live in love is life's greatest challenge. It requires more subtlety, flexibility, sensitivity, understanding, acceptance, tolerance, knowledge, and strength than any other human endeavor or emotion.

—*Leo Buscaglia*

Many of us habitually reject people who show us love. We do this because we fear the love that they can offer us. Rather than finding rapture in someone's love for us, we turn away, as if we're not worthy. But this attitude only brings harm and can injure us deeply. When we harbor a fear of love, we soon find ourselves unhappy and hurt.

On the other hand, by accepting love from others, we can allow love to fill us. But to do this, we must take a big step. We must change something basic. Many of us spend a great deal of time trying to show love to others—trying to find love inside ourselves so that we can bestow it on others. But we neglect to receive the love that is shown us.

Love is a two-way door. We must allow love to enter at least as often as we attempt to give love to others. That's what must change.

So be alert when you are around others. Notice love when it is offered, and allow yourself to receive its energy. As Stephen Levine said: "Nothing is worth the heart being closed, even a moment longer. Nothing. Absolutely nothing."

Try this:

Allow love to enter. When someone shows his or her love to
you, respond positively. Use the moment as your springboard.
It is your opportunity to fly. If you ridicule this person, you lose
it. Drink in the love in all its glory. Let this love fill you.

Accept with enthusiasm the person who shows you love.
When you accept the other unconditionally, the acceptance
itself becomes fulfilling. When you accept the other in love,
your whole being erupts in happiness. Your heart smiles.

Recommended Reading

Love by Leo Buscaglia. New York: Ballantine Books, 1972.
Love Is Letting Go of Fear by Gerald Jampolsky. New York: Bantam,
   1981.
Loving Relationships by Sondra Ray. Berkeley, CA: Celestial Arts,
   1980.

FROM SELF TO OTHERS

To love one's self is the beginning of a life-long romance.

—*Oscar Wilde*

When you were growing up, a well-intentioned parent, older rel-
ative, or teacher probably told you that it was selfish to love yourself. He or she might even have told you that this selfishness would
keep you from learning to love other people.

If you are over the age of twenty, you doubtless heard this at
least once as a child. And if you grew up believing it, you may have
learned to ignore many of your own true feelings when dealing
with others and their feelings. You might even think of yourself as
a martyr, having sacrificed so much for others, and yet you feel
empty inside for all those supposedly selfless favors.

To equate self-love with selfishness is one product of cultural
conditioning that can prevent you from realizing your highest

potential. The self-love referred to here is not vanity, greed, arrogance, or pretentiousness, but feelings of personal goodness and an unconditional acceptance for the person you are. You love yourself when you realize you are an integrated individual who has self-esteem, one who delights in taking care of his or her physical and psychological health. If you have this love, then you can give it to others.

But there's another myth that keeps us from realizing our human potential. It is the belief that love must always have an object. Rather, love functions much like the perfume of a flower, which scents the air whether or not someone is there to savor the aroma. Those with loving natures radiate love wherever they are. Furthermore, they became loving not by sacrificing their personal needs but by enjoying life so fully that they can't help but wish the same enjoyment for others. Their love flows from a joy they've found by being kind to themselves.

Love, then, starts with the self and emanates to other people, plants, and animals. Without this essential goodness, our attempts to love others will fail.

∞ ∞

Try this:

Choose a day when you are relatively free of intrusions and responsibilities. For that day, be your own best friend. Treat yourself royally: make merry, luxuriate in the bathtub, sing, cook yourself a great meal, and enjoy it leisurely. Spend the entire day loving yourself.

Through this kindness, you will come to feel good about yourself, glad to be alive, thankful for your body and mind. If you lavish yourself with love from time to time, you will naturally become more loving toward others.

Recommended Reading

"Song of Myself" from *Leaves of Grass* by Walt Whitman. New York: Vintage Books, 1992.

PART FOUR

Spiritual Peace

To the poet, to the philosopher, to the saint, all things are friendly and sacred, all events profitable, all days holy, all men divine.

—*Ralph Waldo Emerson*

Without the spiritual component of well-being, we cannot integrate our physical, mental, and emotional selves to attain inner peace, for the spiritual determines our prevailing vision of the world. It is through the spiritual that we face those great mysteries: life, death, and God. Our spirituality empowers us. It affects the way we think and feel about ourselves and others as well as the way we work, create, and seek our livelihood. The spiritual is the most intimate part of a human being

We may practice a religion that largely determines our spiritual outlook or we may eschew religion altogether. But our religious beliefs aren't as important as the degree to which we use our faith to live in harmony with ourselves and others. Unfortunately, our convictions about God and heaven can immobilize or stunt our spiritual selves; we will not grow if we think that we will "be saved" simply by believing, without having to act on our beliefs.

On the other hand, when we actively seek to experience and express the divine within ourselves, we make our lives in this world more heavenly. Whatever we can use to spiritualize ourselves becomes a tool to deepen our peace of mind. However, what works for one person may not work for another. Spirituality is a personal affair, and our spiritual growth, if it is genuine, will help us to honor our individual differences. Therefore, tolerance of other people's views and practices is essential to spiritual maturity.

155

Spirituality is an active, dynamic relationship with all living beings and with the earth itself. As you grow spiritually, you develop a sense of the divine that makes you thankful to be alive.

CHAPTER 12

Connecting with God

What a powerful feeling the idea of God brings! There are hundreds of ideas of God and as many ways to bring God into your life. What is your conception of God? Perhaps you see God in a certain form, such as that of a man (like the Christian image of God the Father), a woman (like Isis or some other goddess), an animal (like the totemic Eagle of native American worship), or a specific historical figure (like Christ or Buddha). Perhaps you perceive God as formless, as an impersonal force inherent in all creation. Your conception of God is as valid as anyone's as long as it isn't used as a vehicle for intolerance and fanaticism. (Then it is destructive.)

Your image of God actually has little to do with your relationship to God. But the more lovingly devoted you are to your image of God, the deeper your connection with inner peace.

This chapter explores how to use images of God to deepen your love.

HEAVEN WITHIN

What a pity that the only way to heaven is in a hearse!
—*Stanislaw J. Lec*

It seems that we've gone a long way to distance ourselves from heaven. We've done this in the name of religion, and done ourselves a vast disservice. The notion that we must wait until we die to enter a paradise we've never seen is often used as an excuse to postpone finding happiness on earth. The belief in a beatific afterlife, in which all our needs are met, can—like all beliefs—restrain our inner growth. It is one thing to believe in something and strive to learn whether it is true and quite another to rest contentedly with a belief, thinking that it alone is enough to ensure a future of eternal happiness.

All the great spiritual figures in history have said the same thing in their individual ways. What they have said is: Heaven lies within you. You don't need to believe in a glorious afterlife or wait until you are dead to experience a deep, fulfilling peace. Many of these teachers have also said that this world is the only heaven you can ever know and that you have been given the gift of a human life to realize this. What's the message? Seek fulfillment now, on this earth, in this lifetime.

Our spiritual leaders have tried to teach us to look within ourselves for the pearl of serenity, claiming that it exists within everyone, just as it did within them. What's more, when we find this serenity, this heaven within, we see that the world is heavenly, too.

Of course, this doesn't mean that we become Pollyannas, blind to injustice and suffering, but that we have a greater appreciation for life as we find it and that we are intent on leading kind, peaceful, and caring lives, regardless of the circumstances we face. This can be a realistic, not an idealistic, paradise. All you need to do is put it into practice.

∞ ∞

Try this:

Sit quietly and close your eyes. Silently say to yourself, "Heaven lies within me." Let this be an affirmation. Feel it working in the region of your heart. Focus your awareness there as if it is a new world you are entering. Go deep inside this world until your body is absolutely still. Surrender to the feeling of inner peace.

Before getting up, tell yourself that you will take this peace with you wherever you go. The afterglow of your experience will stay with you for several hours. Furthermore, in times of stress, you will remember the heaven within, and it will help you to face the world with a renewed serenity.

Recommended Reading

Practice of the Presence of God by Brother Lawrence. Mount Vernon, New York: Peter Pauper Press, 1967.

FINDING YOUR OWN PERSONAL GOD

It is the heart which experiences God, and not the reason.

—*Blaise Pascal*

There is a story about a Hindu sage who radiated a palpable sense of peace and love to all those in his presence. One day the sage was visited by a poor farmer who lamented that he felt no love for God. He had no heart for worship and found religious observances meaningless. At the same time, he wished he were devout and believed that the spiritual sense he lacked would make him a happier man. In short, he yearned to see God even though he didn't believe in God.

"Forget God," the sage told him. "What do you love?"

The farmer was bewildered. He looked at the sage and stammered, "I . . . I don't know."

"Come, come," said the sage, "you must love something. Now think, think what it is you love."

The farmer thought about it. At last he said, "I am very poor, my beloved wife is dead, and I have no children. Life has dealt me many hard blows. All that I own besides my hut and an acre of land is a cow. I guess I love my cow. Other than her, I can't think of one thing I love."

"If you love your cow," said the sage, "then your cow is God. Go and worship your cow."

When the farmer left, he could not help thinking that the sage's advice was crazy. My cow is God? How ridiculous! Nevertheless, he was at his wit's end, having lived a squalid life in which he barely earned enough to eat and keep a roof over his head. Without a wife, children, and a sense of God, he was unhappy and lonely and couldn't imagine feeling more miserable. So he decided to give this harebrained scheme a try. What did he have to lose? He would see if there was any logic to the holy man's madness.

"All right, God," he said to his emaciated cow as she grazed on a patch of parched grass. "Show me your stuff! Speak to me! Give me some words of wisdom!"

Of course, the cow said nothing but only glanced at the farmer with a hungry look in her eyes. He noticed, then, what a scrawny beast she was. He went into his hut and cooked a bowl of rice and lentils and brought it to the cow. As the cow ate the food —a welcome change from the parched grass—the farmer knelt before her in an attitude of prayer. Wait! Were the neighbors watching? He looked furtively about and, seeing that the coast was clear, brought the palms of his hands together and gazed at the cow, remembering the love he once felt for his young wife.

Each day after that, when he wasn't working, he spent his time feeding his cow homemade meals and kneeling reverently before her as she ate. He gazed at this creature, summoning the affection he had for his wife when he was happily married. He petted the cow and thanked her for being alive. At night, instead of retiring to his hut, he slept outside in the field, beside the cow.

After a month of this, he returned to the sage. "I can't believe it," said the farmer. "I feel blessed to have my cow. I love her as much as I loved my wife. I sing praises to my cow each morning and each night. Oh, I'm sure they aren't devout by your standards and I don't have much of a voice, but it does my heart so much good to sing to my cow. And when I'm away from her, in the village or working in the far corner of my field, I see my cow before me, in the sheaves of wheat I grow, in the villagers' faces, in the sky —everywhere! I feel like a new man!"

This story illustrates an important principle for those of us who aren't particularly religious yet wish to have a more reverent sense of life. If you find no personal meaning in the symbols, doc-trines, and practices of institutions, but you want to experience your devotional nature and those loving feelings that bring joy and peace of mind, you can follow the example of the poor farmer. Now there's no need to rush out and buy a cow! Instead, ask your-self what it is you love and then open your heart to your own beloved. It may be your calico cat or your loyal English setter or garden-variety mongrel who likes to sleep by your feet. It may be a friend or child, the potted geranium in your bedroom or flow-ering forsythia bush in your yard. It may be the photograph of a departed loved one or a picture of a stranger who projects a capti-vating serenity and grace. Whatever or whoever stirs a loving sense in your heart is worthy of your adoration, just as the cow was for the farmer.

Love, that most relaxing energy, is a personal affair. Forcing yourself to love something to which you don't relate is, in a sense, to deny your individuality. Human beings are as unique as snow-flakes, and each of us must honor his or her own inclinations. Otherwise we are wasting our time and working against heartfelt impulses.

If God is love, then what you love is the embodiment of God. That is the essence of the story of the farmer and his cow. Each of us must find his or her own cow in order to cultivate our loving natures and begin to experience a sense of the divine and the serene gratitude that accompanies this sense. What you love is a spring-board to spiritual insight, a tangible means to the realm of the sacred.

☞ ☞

Try this:

Ask yourself what awakens your deepest affection. If you need to, make a list of the creatures and things you love, and select the item that most inspires your gratitude. Then spend some time each day with that person, animal, plant, or object. Whatever you have selected, the test of its capacity to evoke your love is this: while in its presence, you should feel relaxed and uninhibited.

Once you're sure this is the case, gaze calmly at whatever you have chosen and imagine a path or taproot connecting your eyes to your heart. Let your seeing be from the heart, and if you can touch the object, imagine your hand connected to your heart.

This exercise may be easier if you have chosen something other than a person as your beloved (an exception might be an infant). Unless you have a partner, friend, or lover who is agreeable and available, you are better off choosing someone or something with whom you do not feel at all self-conscious. If your love object is a pet, spend time stroking its body. This will calm you as well as the animal. (It's a medically confirmed fact that petting a friendly cat or dog lowers one's blood pressure.) The main thing is to use your senses of sight and touch affectionately by putting your heart into them.

If you faithfully practice this exercise, you will soon experience a melting sensation in the region of your heart and a relaxed sense of being. As a result, you will be more at peace with yourself and with the world.

Recommended Reading

The Mythic Imagination: Your Quest for Meaning through Personal Mythology by Stephen Larsen, Ph.D. New York: Bantam, 1990.

GOD WITH A FACE

We should find God in what we do know, not in what we don't.
—*Dietrich Bonhoeffer*

Perhaps for you the word *God* is devoid of meaning. That is, when you think of God, you can't associate the thought with an image that affects you one way or another. Or you may be a person for whom the word *God* is closely associated with a human being who personifies all the great virtues you associate with spirituality.

Regardless of your religious or spiritual training, you may be a practical person who relates well to concrete images and doesn't like abstractions.

A concrete image carries power because it doesn't rely on explanations or words to elicit an emotional response, provided the viewer is sympathetic to the image. One of the most powerful images is a picture or photograph of the human face.

It has been said that the face indicates the soul. Perhaps you cannot imagine the soul—the mysterious force that animates your body and mind. Maybe you don't even believe in the soul. But few people can look at the face of someone who is happy and deeply at peace and not feel either envious or inspired.

If you feel a tangible image could awaken your human potential, you have a ready means to inner peace. The following experiments use images to develop peace of mind.

∽ ∽

Try this:

1. *Contemplate a good face.*   Find some photographs of individuals whom you revere. These may be famous people or personal loved ones. Study your photographs closely. Be sure that the people you choose are not merely charismatic personalities of popular culture, but individuals who evoke in you feelings of peace, goodness, happiness, and love. The key to selection is that the person's face should inspire you and make you want to emulate him or her. Read about this individual's life. Many have lived noble, creative lives, and their faces reflect this experience. Whether or not you are religious in the traditional sense, there are plenty of people to choose from. Here are some suggestions: Mother Teresa, Walt Whitman, Albert Schweitzer, Mahatma Gandhi, Ramana Maharshi, Rainer Maria Rilke, Leo Tolstoy, Elisabeth Kübler-Ross, Thich Nhat Hahn, William Blake, Albert Einstein, Krishnamurti, D.T. Suzuki, the Dalai Lama, Thomas Merton, Vaslav Nijinsky, Ram Dass.

Place the photograph you've selected on the wall in your
room. Sit quietly before the photo, and study the person's features. See the happiness, the experience of inner peace animating
his or her eyes and emanating from the flesh. Let yourself be in a
sympathetic mood. Summon a feeling of deep admiration for this
person. Imagine yourself taking on his or her characteristics:
mental contentment, compassion, creativity, joy. Gaze at the
picture for at least ten minutes, feeling yourself absorbing the
power and radiance of your mentor's face. Then close your eyes
and see the image in your mind. Allow your own inner beauty to
emerge as you meditate on this image.

2. *Create a shrine.*   This method works well for followers
of traditional religions. Surround an area of your room with
pictures of the proponents of your religion or spiritual path.
These might be pictures of Christ, Buddha, Moses, Sufi mystics,
Zen masters, native American visionaries such as Black Elk, or
Hindu saints and yogis. Create a shrine in the corner of your
bedroom, and sit before the inspiring pictures you have chosen.
Be still as you gaze at them, absorbing the attributes of the
spiritual individuals who inspire you. After a while, close your
eyes and experience the peace that comes from following your
sacred path.

3. *Contemplate a symbol.*   If you respond more to symbols
than faces, try meditating on the symbol that inspires you most.
It may be a beautiful painting, such as Matisse's *The Joy of Life*, or
a complex but harmonious Tibetan mandala. It may be a cross,
a star, or a photograph of the earth taken from the moon. Whatever it is, it must awaken in you feelings of peace and reverence
for life. Meditate on this symbol, and enjoy the spiritual growth
it brings.

Recommended Reading

A Book of Angels by Sophy Burnham. New York: Ballantine Books,
    1990.

GOD WITHOUT A FACE

There is a sort of transcendental ventriloquy through which men can be made to believe that something which was said on earth came from heaven.

—*G. C. Lichtenberg*

What is God to you? No matter what God you seek, you cannot find your God in words. You will not find God in a text or scripture.

Words act as signposts only. They can show you the way to God, but they cannot show you God. You won't find God even in the word *God* as much as you might utter it with great solemnity. The word will not produce the thing it represents. Indeed, when God appears, there is no word to describe the phenomenon. All words disappear in the experience.

What happens when God appears? What kind of experience is it? Words can't describe it, but with words we can create an idea of it. One thing can be said for sure: the experience of God varies according to who you are. People experience God differently. For many people, particularly the scientifically minded, the experience brings a feeling of connectedness with everything.

Experiencing God makes you feel connected within yourself and connected with the world. The French poet Lamartine said, "God is but a word used to explain the world." And, remember, you are intimately a part of the world. God, as world, encompasses everything, including you. It exists within you and without you. In fact, the world and you are one. So rather than seeking to transcend this world, seek to know it intimately.

But that's not easy, is it? The world is so mundane. The world consists of everyday things scattered all around you—toasters, carrots, automobiles, pet rabbits, and stars at night. How can you be one with all that?

Yet you *are* one with everything because everything in the universe is made of the same stuff. The same matter that constitutes you constitutes toasters, carrots, automobiles, pet rabbits, and stars at night. The building blocks of the universe are the same for everything within it.

∞ ∞

Try this:

Consider your oneness with everything. Meditate on it. Say to yourself, "I am one with all there is." When you understand this, you begin to show reverence for the world around you, for the cosmic forces inside and outside of you.

Reverence, a profoundly beautiful emotion, leads to inner peace. How do you develop this beautiful emotion?

Reverence starts with a realization about the world that leads to wonder or awe. You realize basically that you are one with everything. Whatever is God is in you as well as outside of you. You can find no separation. In addition, you see that God is the same for everything that exists, from the tiniest particle to the broadest expanse in space.

When you grasp this simple wonder of the universe, you begin to feel appreciation. Specifically, you appreciate your connectedness with all that is. And you melt into it. This gratitude is reverence. Really, reverence is an internal thank-you for the world as it is.

A passage from Heinrich Zimmer's book *The Philosophies of India* may help you to visualize the sense of awe that leads to reverence. (Women should feel free to read the fourth sentence as, "I am Woman, the Goddess" or "I am Woman, the Lord.")

> I am smaller than the minutest atom, likewise greater than the greatest. I am the whole, the diversified-multi-colored-lovely-strange universe. I am the Ancient One. I am Man, the Lord. I am the Being-of-Gold. I am the very state of divine beatitude.

CHAPTER 13

Sex

*I*f we approach it reverently and playfully, sex leads directly to inner peace. When we have reverence for our partners, sex elevates us with loving feelings. And when we have a playful attitude, our sensuality becomes a delight.

In the Eastern spiritual tradition, there is a term, *leela*, that means "divine playfulness" and equates spirituality with fun. The idea of *leela* applies especially to sex, because sex, if used the right way, is a means to spiritual ecstasy.

You must put aside all your anticipations as you enter the sexual act. For when you engage in sex with no thought of orgasm, no expectations, and no preconceived goal, you can experience the melting warmth between you and your partner that transforms physical lust into the deepest experience of love imaginable.

YOUR LOVER AS THE BELOVED

The sexual embrace can only be compared with music and with prayer.

—*Havelock Ellis*

Sex has a vast power for awakening inner peace, but we tend to misuse its power. We limit ourselves with our vision of sex, and this vision is limited by a long history of cultural conditioning. At

167

one extreme is the puritanical mind, which considers sex dirty and animalistic; at the other extreme is the perverted, pornographic mind, which also views sex as dirty but greedily craves it. For both mind-sets, sex is a form of bondage.

If you feel that your sex life has become monotonous and unsatisfactory, you might begin to look for new types of experiences or other potential partners. If you are married or in a relationship, you might want to have a fling or find a new lover to bring you out of your doldrums. In our restless country where people change residences on an average of once every three years and two out of three marriages end in divorce, we spend much time trying to escape our situations and circumstances. The grass is always greener on the other side of the fence.

But do you need a new relationship, a new partner, or a new spouse to make your sex life fulfilling? Or do you need a new vision of your present relationship?

A healthy sex life can do much to make you feel at peace with yourself and with your lover. It starts with a mutual willingness. Sexual fulfillment depends on your willingness to satisfy your partner and his or her willingness to satisfy you. Achieving this willingness requires an element of surrender. Without it you remain trapped in self-consciousness or hung up about having your desires met in a particular way. If they are not met in this way, you become frustrated and angry; you may even blame your partner for his or her sexual ineptitude or lack of sensitivity. In this situation, the sexual act will become mechanical and no longer a source of intense pleasure.

What is usually needed is not a change of partners but a change in attitude. You must bring a new vision to the sexual act itself. By dropping your expectations and conditioning, you can enrich your sexual life and deepen your relationship with your partner.

∞ ∞

Try this:

1. *Talk.*   Discuss your need to revitalize your sex life with your lover or mate. Chances are, he or she feels the same way

you do, especially if the pleasure you get from the act has been waning or unsatisfactory. Agree that the two of you will make love only when you really want to. Agree that you will not use sex as a way to reduce contention or patch up misunderstandings, since this merely diminishes its energy. Agree to enter the sex act consciously and to bring to it awareness and sensitivity. Finally, agree not to make love when either one of you is tired, depressed, or distraught.

2. *Ritual.* Before making love, light a candle and burn incense or use one of the fragrances available as aromatherapy. Creating a relaxing and sensuously stimulating environment can set the stage for beautiful lovemaking.

Sit or lie down together, join hands, and gaze into each other's eyes. As you share this mutual gaze, breathe deeply and in harmony until both of you feel relaxed. By doing this, you and your partner will blend your energies and feel a vital exchange. Take your time; there is no reason to rush. Let this act be a ritual in the true sense of that word: a ceremonial act designed to awaken your consciousness.

3. *Surrender.* Once you feel the merging of energies, caress each other slowly. You can also start by massaging each other, using a natural scented oil for lubrication. Massage is an excellent way to relax and blend your energies even more.

Then let your intuition take over, and surrender to your lover. The way to surrender is to view your lover as a divine being, as divine as you are, with the same potential for ecstasy and inner peace. Then give your entire being to this divine being.

Move slowly as you engage in your lovemaking, attuned to all your bodily senses. It may help if you think of playing your lover's body as if it were a musical instrument. At the same time, don't focus on orgasm. Try to forget your former notions and habits. Focus on being loving and caring yet playful. Don't take the act seriously. Don't strain. Don't be obsessed. Set no goals.

Allow yourself a month to experiment with making love this way. At the end of that time, compare your new way of loving with your former way. Ask your partner to tell you his or her feelings. Which way is more fulfilling? Which way ensures a greater harmony with your partner?

Recommended Reading

Challenge of the Heart: Love, Sex, and Intimacy in Changing Times edited by John Welwood. Boston: Shambhala, 1985.
Sexual Secrets: The Alchemy of Ecstasy by Nik Douglas and Penny Slinger. New York: Destiny Books, 1979.

BECOME THE ENERGY

> *Sex is innocent energy—life flowing in you, Existence alive in you. Do not cripple it! Allow it to move toward the heights.*
> —Bhagwan Shree Rajneesh

Sex stirs our deepest, most beautiful energy. It connects us to life itself. As two beings become one in the communion of sex, a door opens. It is the door to heaven.

Of course, this is not true of any kind of sex but only deeply relaxed sex that is uninhibited by religious ideology and unencumbered by thoughts. To make you whole, sex must be total. Total sex means there's no mind involved. In total sex, the mind disappears.

Typically, in sex, the mind wants to identify. ("Who's this person I'm with?") The mind wants to pass judgment. ("Maybe this is not the right thing.") The mind wants to ask questions. ("Am I doing OK?" "Is it good for you?") And the mind wants to make comparisons. ("Is she or he physically more appealing than so-and-so?")

Also, many of us were brought up to fear sex or feel guilty about it. As children, we may have heard: "Don't touch there, it's dirty," "Don't do that, it's bad," or "It's wrong." We may have been inappropriately touched by someone, and the memory of this experience inhibits us sexually. Today we hear "Don't do it, you may get AIDS," instilling yet another fear about having sex.

In order to feel free in sex and fully appreciate it, we must drop the fear and the guilt. Take the time to choose a partner carefully, and to prevent disease and unwanted pregnancy. But after that, it's all systems go. During the act itself, we need to drop all thoughts. We need to release our minds and become our bodies. Only then can sex be ecstatic.

How can you release the mind? Allow the sexual energy full rein in your body. Let its vibrant power take over. When you do, there's no room for the mind to enter. If you become the energy itself, the mind will neither disturb nor distract you.

The six techniques in this section are invaluable because they can help you to enter sex fully, and once you learn to do this, you'll feel joyously in harmony with your body. Sex will then release the life force within you in the form of love.

Without the mind involved, sex becomes a profoundly peaceful experience. When there's no need to hurry, you will simply linger in the moment—and linger and linger, as you melt into love.

∞ ∞

Try this:

1. Become the body. Don't think, do.
2. Become the kiss. Don't think of yourself as the person giving the kiss or the person receiving the kiss; think of yourself as the kiss itself. In the same way, become the embrace, become the sexual act itself. Become the motion.
3. Slow the motion. What's your hurry?
4. Melt together. Visualize becoming one with your partner by letting yourself melt into him or her. As you connect together sexually, become one person rather than two.
5. Remain in the middle. When you feel drawn to excitement, wait. Do not move to the excitement, let it come to you.
   By practicing this, you can remain fully relaxed while fully aroused.

6. Imagine losing yourself completely. Love is giving, so practice
   this in sex. Practice giving yourself away. Your whole body
   will be like rippling waves of loving energy.

Recommended Reading

The Art of Sexual Ecstasy by Margo Annand. Los Angeles: Jeremy P.
     Tarcher, 1989.
The Book of Secrets by Bhagwan Shree Rajneesh. New York: Harper
     & Row, 1974.
The Tao of Love and Sex by Jolan Chang. London: Wildwood
     House, 1977.

CHAPTER 14

Acceptance

*T*oo often, the easiest word to say is no. We use it to resist the world. But with our ongoing resistance, we deny ourselves and restrict our creative energy. The more we fight with the world, the more tension we build in ourselves.

Pain is part of the process of life. However much we try to avoid pain and cling to pleasure, we will never succeed. In fact, our attempts at this actually increase our suffering and mental anguish whenever life doesn't meet our expectations.

But when we give up this struggle and accept the world as it is, no longer resisting the pain of life, we become more at peace with ourselves and with the world.

In this chapter, you'll learn to put aside your likes and dislikes. You'll discover how relaxing it is to face life wholeheartedly.

ACCEPTING THE WORLD AS IT IS

We read the world wrong and say that it deceives us.

—Rabindranath Tagore

Have you ever noticed that when you get angry you justify your anger, but when someone else gets angry you criticize that person? Most of us have a double standard: one behavioral code for our-

173

selves and another for everyone else. This double standard is a source of inner turmoil because it always judges and always contradicts itself. With this outlook, whatever is wrong exists in others and whatever is right exists in you. The world needs to be changed, but you don't. It follows that you waste a lot of energy complaining about people and things because they don't meet your expectations. If this criticism turns into a mental habit, you keep yourself from experiencing the deep inner peace that comes from accepting life as it is.

Acceptance is one of the most powerful methods for achieving peace of mind. Unfortunately, people are conditioned to reject, criticize, and condemn. But once you realize that greed, rage, hatred, and other dark feelings exist in you as well as in others, you have gone a long way toward transforming these negative energies into the power of inner peace.

Rejection never transforms anything. It simply suppresses. Still worse, anything you suppress becomes more powerful. It moves to your roots, settles in your unconscious, and festers there. But by accepting yourself as a human being with all the faults and problems of other human beings, you will bring these suppressions to the surface, where you can transform them into vital energy.

⌒ ⌒

Try this:

Spend one day accepting people for what they are. Don't condemn them for their actions. Instead, see yourself reflected in whomever you meet. This will bring many of your suppressed thoughts into your conscious mind so that you become aware of them.

For this one day, accept your humanity, your animality, your greed, your anger, and all the other qualities you have denied or justified in yourself by condemning other people. Whatever you feel arise in you through this acceptance, be aware of it without judgment, self-consciousness, or criticism. If greed comes up, don't try to turn it into the absence of greed, or you will suppress it once again. Rather, accept the world and yourself fully, calmly, without any effort to change them.

Encounter life as it unfolds during this day, remembering that reality doesn't exist to meet your expectations. Don't be bothered if you experience a number of feelings you did not know were in you. Think of it this way: if you did not know you had a disease, you would have less chance of being cured. So when negative thoughts surface, face them calmly and don't cling to them, for this is essential to the process of your emotional cleansing.

Acceptance is transformation, because acceptance makes awareness possible. Keep this in mind as you spend an entire day in the attitude of acceptance.

Very likely you will be amazed. You will see how much energy you expend on judgment and criticism. You will see how you deplete yourself by denouncing people, the world, and circumstances—none of which you have the power to change. Furthermore, you will see that the energy you put into complaining about life can be used to deepen your peace.

ACCEPTING DEATH IN LIFE

> I chatter, chatter, as I flow,
> To join the brimming river,
> For men may come and men may go,
> But I go on forever.
>
> —Alfred, Lord Tennyson, "The Brook"

Have you ever thought about your own death? Does thinking about it make you fearful? Most of us do shrink from death. It's a common fear.

In one sense, however, there is no such thing as death. First of all, every living thing has its origin in nonliving things, in things that are essentially dead. Life began through combinations of inorganic matter (earth, air, water, and sunlight), and through these combinations, life continues. All life comes from something that is not life, and this something endures forever.

Also, are you familiar with the cycle of life? Living things eat other living things in order to survive. Thus, as living things die, they become food. In this sense, individual beings die only that others may live.

So, looking at life as a whole, your death means that something else may live. This is the beauty of death. But most religions have destroyed or distorted this beauty and put fear in its place.

Consider how we deal with the end of life. When death occurs, we hide the body in a box—the more permanent the box, the better, the more airtight, the better. Or we burn the body, converting it quickly to smoke and ashes. These methods keep the body from returning to other life. It would be better to bury the body naked in the ground or drop the body into the sea. The body would thus return to life as other living things took it within themselves as food.

This is what we can call "life after death." Our religions have gotten it partly right by asserting that there's some kind of life after death. So here's the first important point to remember: Nothing dies. Life turns into death, death turns into life, but something always exists, something of you exists forever.

Then who dies? Your ego dies. All mental constructs die. Your ego is a mental construct, a created person that is not in any way permanent. All thoughts die, and all knowledge dies, including knowledge of God, Christ, Buddha, the Scriptures, philosophy, life and death, right and wrong, good and bad, your phone number, and your address. All gone.

That leaves you with a body, most of which is food, but the bones—oh the bones—could live on a thousand years, a hundred thousand years, perhaps even a million years. The part of you that lives in your bones will live on and on.

But ego dies. This is the second important thing to remember. If you use meditation techniques to drop the ego, to dissociate yourself from ego, then who dies? No one! There is no one to die. So one way to achieve peacefulness concerning death is to drop the ego now, while you're still alive. Then you cannot die. As Niet-

zsche said, "One must pay dearly for immortality; one has to die
several times while still alive."

At death, your thoughts disappear and all that's left is your
physical being. Yet the physical being gradually transforms into
energy. All of you—everything that is you at death—will become
energy. How beautiful! Walt Whitman described this immortality
in these lines of verse: "All goes onward and outward, nothing col-
lapses, / And to die is different from what anyone supposed, and
luckier."

Try this:

1. *Lie down as dead.*   Breathe deeply for a few moments until
you feel calm. Then forget your breath and stop moving. Drop all
thoughts as if you were dead. Try spending fifteen minutes to a half
hour on this three or four nights a week, and notice how your perspective on life begins to change.

2. *Contemplate death as the ultimate liberation.*   Freedom comes
through death, for when you die you're no longer chained to the
necessities of life, to things such as air, water, food, warmth, and
self-protection. That's why death can be perceived as eternal rest.
It's like a deep sleep from which you never wake. Viewing death as
a kind of liberation will help to free you while you're still alive.
Meditate on this.

3. *Reach for immortality.*   Only the ego dies, so drop the ego
now. Then no one dies. Then you feel immortal while still living.
Then you live in the eternal present.

Another option is to view immortality knowing that something of you lives on. In the matter-energy continuum, what is
currently you simply transforms into something else at death.
Everything changes. You move from the physical plane to a plane
of pure energy or divine light.

A third option is to view immortality with the knowledge
that your ideas and thoughts will remain among the living. They
will be passed from generation to generation, so you can hope to

leave behind some wisdom or fond memories for your kin or for posterity.

4. *View life as if from death.*   In death, would you be afraid of life? Before you were conceived in the womb, do you think you feared coming into life? If not, why should you be afraid of death now? Why bother to fear it during life? Your fear is of no use. Consider this story about a Zen master:

> An ex-emperor asked the master Gudo, "What happens to a man of enlightenment after death?" Gudo replied, "How should I know?" The ex-emperor said, "Why? Because you are a master." Gudo said, "Yes, sir, but not a dead one."

Live now. This is your chance to know life. Wait until you're dead to be concerned with death.

You may want to spend some time imagining how peaceful it was before you were conceived in the womb. This will help you to understand what it's like to be dead. There is no thought and no conflict in death. Now allow your concept of this utter peace to inspire you in life.

5. *Realize that life and death are one.*   Life changes to death, death changes to life; the cycle goes on and on. It's inevitable. Seneca says, "You will die not because you're ill but because you're alive." Life and death are flip sides of the same coin. Instead of life and death, think in terms of matter and energy. Matter changes to energy, energy changes back to matter. Nothing is ever lost. Nothing dies.

Recommended Reading

Easy Death by Da Avabhasa. Clearlake, CA: Dawn Horse Press, 1991.

On Death and Dying by Elisabeth Kübler-Ross. New York: Macmillan, 1970.

Who Dies? by Stephen Levine. New York: Doubleday, 1982.

The Grass Grows by Itself by Bhagwan Shree Rajneesh. Poona, India: Rajneesh Foundation, 1976.

SAYING YES TO LIFE

No dynamo, no matter how huge—not even a dynamo of a hundred million dead souls—can combat one man saying Yes!

—*Henry Miller*

Have you ever put off a project at work or at home until you were faced with a deadline? You procrastinate, resisting the very thought of the task, until the time comes when it can no longer wait. Then you throw yourself into the work, perhaps cursing yourself for waiting so long, and try to get it over with as soon as possible. Then, sometimes, though not always, you suddenly find that your resistance is gone and that the work is far more pleasant than you had thought it would be.

Life isn't interesting in and of itself. What makes it interesting is the attention we bring to it. Therefore the best way to make your life interesting is to bring more attention to each experience and task you face. The quality of your attention determines the degree of enjoyment you get from life. If a task tears you in two—one part of you saying, "I hate this," and the other saying, "I must do it!"—you attend to the task in a halfhearted fashion. Your resistance is what makes the work unpleasant. While you are engaged in it, you are fighting with yourself, and this fight leaves you spent, disgruntled, stressed out, and most likely needing twice the time it would have taken to complete the job if you had faced it with an accepting attitude.

Attention is largely an attitude whose strength depends on your ability to accept each situation for what it is and to make the best of it. Saying yes to life acts as a basic catalyst. It can arouse your attention and enthusiasm. An attitude of acceptance can help you to proceed with your life and face unavoidable tasks, responsibilities, and even calamities, knowing that your internal resistance (that screaming no inside you) will only make matters worse. If you listen to the no and give in to its demands, you are denying life.

Acceptance doesn't mean that you must agree with everyone or become the proverbial doormat over which everyone can walk. If you don't need to do something or don't want to do it, don't! There's no sense in agreeing with someone simply to placate that person. You cannot be at peace if you aren't true to yourself. It's important to remain an individual, loyal to your integrity. But when it comes to responsibilities, why drag yourself to them with a negative attitude? Saying yes to life is the best way to free up energy and feel more alive.

∾ ∾

Try this:

1. *Do what you must by saying yes.*   Spend a day doing whatever you usually do — going to work, paying your bills, mowing the lawn, taking care of your children — and give yourself completely to each activity. Tell yourself you will do each thing required of you with your heart and soul. Affirm this silently to yourself before starting each new task. Then throw yourself into it, and don't hold back. Summon all your energy and creative potential as you meet your daily responsibilities. Proceed slowly yet efficiently, moving without strain, as though whatever you are doing is the most important act in the world. Put aside your likes and dislikes so you can accept each task wholeheartedly. Let your resolve override your appraisal.

When you go to bed at the end of this day, note how you feel. Ask yourself whether you've broken through some resistance that you've had for some time. Do you feel pleasantly tired and fulfilled, or do you feel exhausted? How has this day of saying yes affected your energy level, your self-esteem, your plans for tomorrow, your sense of accomplishment, and your relations with others?

2. *Say yes to pleasures.*   Pick a day in which you can spend as much time as possible doing whatever you want to do. Do things you enjoy. Say yes to all the pleasures and leisure activities

you've dreamed of doing. Summon the power of yes as you treat yourself, living out your dreams of a perfect day. One caveat: during this day, make sure you don't indulge in self-abuse through alcohol, overeating, or drugs. At night, take note of how you feel and ask yourself the same questions as for the previous method.

3. *Now do both.*   Try to arrange your daily life to include both pleasures and responsibilities, and try to face, affirm, and accept them all with the same openness and positive feeling.

Saying yes to life can awaken vigor you never dreamed you had. The positive energy you add to your life will soon increase your overall energy level dramatically. As you greet each day with enthusiasm, you will feel fulfilled.

Recommended Reading

Living, Loving & Learning by Leo Buscaglia, Ph.D. New York: Fawcett Columbine, 1982.

COMPASSION

It is the weak who are cruel. Gentleness can only be expected from the strong.

—*Leo Rosten*

Through your compassion, you show kindness to others. But what happens inside of you? When you do a good deed or help someone out, you feel warm inside. Your heart begins to glow. You settle into a few moments of peaceful contentment.

Try it. Not only will you feel better emotionally, you'll become stronger physically. In a study of 2,700 people over a ten-year period, researchers found that doing volunteer work increased life expectancy more than any other activity.

That's not all. By offering a helping hand, you may actually stimulate your own internal healing. In his best-selling book *Love,*

Medicine & Miracles, Dr. Bernie Siegel reports that doing something for someone else boosts immune system activity. Studies show that it may even be one of the best immune system boosters available.

It all comes down to one simple act: giving. You can give some of your time, energy, or the fruits of your labor to help another person. The happiness you create is bound to make you smile.

∽ ∽

Try this:

1. *Show caring and concern for other people.* Devote yourself to others in every way you can. Remember that caring is one of the most rewarding human emotions. A caring life is a beautiful life.

2. *Say yes to others.* As you would say yes to yourself, say yes to those around you. Celebrate others, show enthusiasm with your friends, and, whenever you can, affirm another person's life.

3. *Accept others with all their differences.* Acceptance can be difficult because other people are different from you and will do things that make you angry. When this happens, acknowledge your feelings without giving in to them. How? Take other people for what they are, be thankful for their differences, and revel in the uniqueness of each. After all, the world would be a dull place if everyone were the same. In addition, forgive those who have done you wrong—and do it as soon as possible. Forgiveness helps to dissipate your anger and bring you peace.

4. *Do a good deed.* The Boy Scouts have a powerful slogan: "Do a good deed daily." You may want to make it your slogan, too. Meanwhile, keep another popular slogan in mind: "Helping you helps me."

5. *Be kind.*

Recommended Reading

Peace Is Every Step by Thich Nhat Hanh, 121–126. New York: Bantam, 1991.

Love, Medicine & Miracles by Bernie Siegel. New York: Harper, 1986.

Fire in the Soul by Joan Borysenko, Ph.D., 194–202. New York: Warner Books, 1993.

Random Acts of Kindness by the Editors of Conari Press. Berkeley, CA: Conari Press, 1993.

CHAPTER 15

Gratitude

*I*n Paul Reps's book, *Zen Flesh, Zen Bones*, there is a story that illustrates gratitude:

> Ryokan, a Zen master, lived the simplest kind of life in a little hut at the foot of a mountain. One evening a thief visited the hut only to discover there was nothing in it to steal.

> Ryokan returned and caught him. "You may have come a long way to visit me," he told the prowler, "and you should not return empty-handed. Please take my clothes as a gift."

> The thief was bewildered. He took the clothes and slunk away.

> Ryokan sat naked, watching the moon. "Poor fellow," he mused, "I wish I could give him this beautiful moon."

Can we offer each other the moon?

PRAYER

The path of prayer leads to the center of peace.

—Oscar Wilde

When we pray—if we pray at all—we usually ask for something. This may be a material object, like a new car; a change of circum-

184

stance, such as a new job; or freedom from a craving, addiction, or a bad situation. Generally we use prayer when we feel needy, desperate, or destitute. In fact, studies show that the number of people who pray when feeling good or prosperous or unthreatened by destiny is small compared to the number who pray when things go wrong in their lives.

Too often, prayer is used as a vehicle to fulfill our wishes, hopes, and dreams. When we get to the depths of suffering and hardship, we pray as a last resort, a final grasp at a small chance for change. We use prayer to pound on heaven's doors, with our longing to be released from a misery that seems unbearable. But as the prominent clergyman Harry Emerson Fosdick said, "God is not a cosmic bellboy for whom we can press a button to get things done."

If properly used, prayer can be a powerful aid to inner peace. But we must first take it out of its usual context and explore its roots, its true meaning and purpose. Prayer is a way of communing with the vast universe and the miraculous forces that sustain its existence. To pray with this purpose in mind, you might begin by audibly or silently addressing the supreme power that keeps our earth revolving about the sun and the galaxies of stars and planets in harmony. Your words will act as a vehicle to bring you to that silent place where you feel at one with yourself and the universal forces. Only then can prayer help you to enjoy a happier and more peaceful life regardless of the circumstances you face. Prayer can facilitate your trust in the mysterious power that has given you life, and this trust can help you to meet challenges and take risks.

According to the stages of life development defined by the psychologist Erik Erikson, the last stage of adult growth is "Integrity versus Despair." At this stage, says Erikson, those of us who have developed the willingness to take risks can more easily endure traumas and crises. These adults find that the ultimate disaster of death is not frightening and that the so-called limitations of aging are actually challenges through which we are meant to grow.

Those of us who hide from the challenges and mysteries of life typically regard aging and death as enemies that will eventually destroy what little peace we have. But when we connect with some power that transcends our lives, we can more readily accept the unexpected or the previously denied courses of our destinies. Prayer can help us to do this.

It's fine to pray when you feel lonely, depressed, desperate, or despairing, as long as you realize that God is not at your beck and call. And it's just as good to pray when you feel satisfied or exuberant. Regardless of your current circumstances, praying is a good practice for evoking your acceptance of life and peace of mind.

∞ ∞

Try this:

1. *Trust your intuition.*   This innate knowledge is the best guide you have. When wrestling with a personal problem or dilemma, make a list of all possible solutions. Read the list over once or twice, then stop thinking about it and trust in powers beyond yourself to give you the right answer.

At night, pray for an answer in simple, sincere words, and go to sleep with the firm belief that you will wake up knowing what you must do.

2. *Give thanks for happiness.*   When you feel especially good about life, bring your palms together, bow down, and thank the universe. Let your praise trail off into silence, and surrender everything you know and feel and think about yourself. Enjoy the inner peace that results.

3. *Live prayerfully.*   Select a day in which you do everything, from taking out the garbage to consoling your child, with a sense of reverence. For this special day, let each of your actions be a prayer that honors the essential goodness of life. When you go to bed, take stock of how you feel and decide if you enjoyed this day and would like to spend another like it.

4. *Pray before the night sky.*   Step outside after dark, look up at the sky and its magnificent reach of stars, and surrender to your sense of wonder. Hold your arms wide open as you gaze up and thank the miraculous powers that sustain your life in this sensuous world. After giving thanks, be silent and enjoy the peace that surpasses understanding.

Recommended Reading

Peace Prayers: Meditations, Affirmations, Invocations, Poems, and Prayers for Peace edited by Carrie Leadingham, Joann E. Moschella, and Hilary M. Vartanian. San Francisco: Harper Collins, 1992.

PRAISE

> *Praise is the best diet for us, after all.*
>
> —*Sydney Smith*

When you offer someone praise, you help that person to be at peace. Certainly a kind word can make anybody's day. But here's the most interesting thing: the more you praise others, the more peaceful you will feel. There's built-in feedback: when you instill peace within someone else, you become peaceful too.

If this is so, why do we expend so much energy ridiculing other people and giving them a hard time? Such behavior most likely results from egotism. When you praise someone else, you lift that person above you. So, in that moment at least, you must forget your own ego. In order to exalt the other, you must drop the self.

But in America we're strong, self-centered individuals. We're tough! We want to be superior to others; we want to win. If we praise somebody, everybody wins. We don't want that. It must be "me" who wins. We look out for number one.

This explains why Americans endure so much emotional suffering. Rather than connecting with the world, we worship rugged individualism and strive to become individuals ourselves. But this separates us from one another. And then we feel alone and lonely.

In truth, praise is akin to love. Praise connects you to another human being. Through praise, you show heartfelt gratitude for a person who experiences problems, sufferings, joys, and dreams, just as you do.

∞ ∞

Try this:

As soon as you notice a positive or noble trait in someone, praise him or her for it. Do this frequently. The more you do it, the better you'll feel.

If you have children, praise them. You'll probably find it easier to praise children than adults. That's because children are more open to the world. So practice your praise on children, then work your way up to adults. Adults may get suspicious. They may think you're out to get something, but praise them anyway.

Watch how your relationship changes with each person you praise. Note particularly how often *you* begin to smile.

Keep in mind that when you praise someone, it's best to praise the person outright. Offer the commendation without bringing up any negative thoughts or associations. For instance, you might say to your child, "You really do well getting yourself up for school on time. That's great!" Don't add, "When I was a kid, I could never get up on time. I was always late." Appending a negative thought lessens the positivity embedded in the first statement. It also shifts the perspective to you, the speaker, rather than keeping it solely on the person receiving praise.

When giving praise, concentrate on the other person and on the positive. And notice how good this feels!

THANKFULNESS FOR LIFE

Awakening
in a moment of peace
I give thanks
to the source of all peace.

—*Harriet Kofalk*

Where do we get the smugness that blinds us to the miracle of being alive? Why do we take life for granted? To answer these questions, we must look at ourselves and the way we perceive the world.

To be smug is to be old, regardless of your chronological age. Smugness stultifies your creativity, learning, daringness, and efforts at discovery, and it makes you overlook the joys of life. Those of us who become smug avoid the work of inner growth. We think we know it all when in fact we are jaded and cynical and unwilling to explore our human potential. As Harry Emerson Fosdick said, "Watch what people are cynical about, and one can often discover what they lack."

One of the best ways to shake off complacence and revive an enthusiasm for life is to develop our sense of gratitude. The following excerpt from a poem by Thich Nhat Hanh shows how gratitude makes one feel more alive.

Waking up this morning, I see the blue sky
I join my hands in thanks for the many wonders of life,
For having twenty-four brand new hours.
The sun is rising on the forest
and so is my awareness.

Thankfulness for life opens us to a sense of wonder and heightens our awareness. We feel the wonder and awareness of being alive in a human body that breathes and walks and perceives the beauty of the earth and the gift of time.

Most of us want to express our joy at being alive, but few of us realize that we can best express this through gratitude. If you are thankful for life, you don't need to look for any other blessing.

∞ ∞

Try this:

When you wake up tomorrow, tell yourself that you are grateful for what you have. You're grateful for the body in which you live and move and work. You're grateful for another day in which to live. Spend time enjoying your breakfast, sipping your tea or coffee, savoring your food, fully indulging your sense of taste. Notice how this sensuous appreciation makes you feel. Take time to look out the window at the sun, sky, and trees. Drink in and savor what you see, for it too is nourishment that will satisfy your essential hunger for life. Allow yourself to be surprised, to give thanks, and to praise. Notice beautiful things you've taken for granted or overlooked. Open your eyes and see them. Then thank each separate thing for being a part of your life. Do the same with your loved ones, children, friends, and the other people around you. You needn't verbalize your appreciation out loud, but silently give thanks for all the blessings you have. Finally, give thanks for your own body, your own breath.

Recommended Reading

Chop Wood, Carry Water by Rick Fields, with Peggy Taylor, Rex Weyler, and Rick Ingrasci. Los Angeles: Jeremy P. Tarcher, 1984.

Our Appointment with Life: The Buddha's Teaching on Living in the Present by Thich Nhat Hanh. Berkeley, California: Parallax Press, 1990.

Afterword

Congratulations! By using the methods in this book, you have achieved greater peace of mind. We encourage you to continue practicing those methods that help you to remain calm and peaceful, cheerful and energetic.

Now, if you have a moment, we'd like to hear from you. Over the years we have worked with hundreds of individuals, using various methods to help them achieve inner peace. We have developed what we think is the best program to meet everyone's needs. But please tell us how well the program worked for you. Which methods worked best for you? What ideas do you have to help us improve this book?

In addition, if you would like help with a specific problem or if you want us to answer questions you have, we're available. We'll respond by mail as soon as possible.

Please write to us: Jerry Dorsman and Bob Davis
c/o New Dawn, Inc.
28 Cherokee Drive
Newark, DE 19713

Bibliography

Ackerman, Diane. *A Natural History of the Senses*. New York: Vintage Books, 1991.

Alberti, Robert, Ph.D., and Emmons, Michael L., Ph.D. *Your Perfect Right: A Guide to Assertive Living*. San Luis Obispo, CA: Impact Publishers, 1990.

Annand, Margo. *The Art of Sexual Ecstasy*. Los Angeles: Jeremy P. Tarcher, Inc., 1989.

Badiner, Allan Hunt (editor). *Dharma Gaia: A Harvest of Essays in Buddhism and Ecology*. Berkeley, CA: Parallax Press, 1990.

Becker, Robert O., M.D., and Selden, Gary. *The Body Electric: Electromagnetism and the Foundation of Life*. New York: Morrow, 1985.

Beinfield, Harriet, L.Ac., and Korngold, Efrem, L.Ac., O.M.D. *Between Heaven and Earth: A Guide to Chinese Medicine*. New York: Ballantine Books, 1991.

Bennett, J.G. *Transformation*. Charles Town, WV: Claymont Communications, 1978.

Bhakti, Sara, Ph.D. *Listening with the Heart: And Other Communication Skills*. Santa Cruz, CA: Gaea Center, 1991.

Bilodeau, Lorraine, M.S. *The Anger Workbook*. Minneapolis, MN: Compcare Publishers, 1992.

Bloomfield, Harold H., M.D., with Felder, Leonard, Ph.D. *Making Peace with Yourself: Turning Your Weaknesses into Strengths*. New York: Ballantine Books, 1985.

Borysenko, Joan, Ph.D. *Fire in the Soul*. New York: Warner Books, 1993.

Brunton, Paul. *The Secret Path*. New York: E. P. Dutton, 1935.

Burnham, Sophy. *A Book of Angels*. New York: Ballantine Books, 1990.

Buscaglia, Leo, Ph.D. *Living, Loving & Learning*. New York: Fawcett Columbine, 1982.

Buscaglia, Leo, Ph.D. *Love*. New York: Fawcett Crest, 1972.

Campbell, Joseph. *Myths to Live By*. New York: Bantam, 1972.

Campbell, Joseph with Moyers, Bill. *The Power of Myth*. New York: Doubleday, 1988.

Capra, Fritzof. *The Tao of Physics*. Berkeley, CA: Shambhala, 1975.

Chang, Jolan. *The Tao of Love and Sex: The Ancient Chinese Way to Ecstasy*. New York: E. P. Dutton, 1977.

Cheng, Man-Ching and Smith, Robert W. *T'ai Chi: The Supreme Ultimate Exercise for Health, Sport and Self-Defense*. Rutland, VT: Tuttle, 1965.

Chopra, Deepak, M.D. *Perfect Health: The Complete Mind/Body Guide*. New York: Harmony Books, 1991.

Colbin, Annemarie. *Food and Healing*. New York: Ballantine Books, 1986.

Conari Press Editors. *Random Acts of Kindness*. Berkeley, CA: Conari Press, 1993.

Da Avabhasa. *Easy Death*. Clearlake, CA: Dawn Horse Press, 1991.

David, Marc. *Nourishing Wisdom*. New York: Bell Tower, 1991.

Deng, Ming-Dao. *The Wandering Taoist*. New York: Harper and Row, 1983.

Douglas, Nik and Slinger, Penny. *Sexual Secrets: The Alchemy of Ecstasy*. New York: Destiny Books, 1979.

Dufty, William. *Sugar Blues*. New York: Warner Books, 1975.

Epstein, Edward Jay. *News from Nowhere*. New York: Vintage Books, 1974.

Ferguson, Marilyn. *The Aquarian Conspiracy: Personal and Social Transformation in the 1980's*. Los Angeles: Tarcher, 1980.

Feuerstein, George and Bodian, Stephan (editors). *Living Yoga: A Comprehensive Guide for Daily Life*. New York: Tarcher/Perigee, 1993.

Fields, Rick, with Taylor, Peggy; Weyler, Rex and Ingrasci, Rick. *Chop Wood, Carry Water*. Los Angeles: Jeremy P. Tarcher, 1984.

Finch, Robert and Elder, John (editors). *The Norton Book of Nature Writing*. New York: W. W. Norton, 1990.

Franck, Frederick. *The Awakened Eye: A Companion Volume to the Zen of Seeing/Drawing as Meditation*. New York: Vintage Books, 1979.

Franck, Frederick. *The Zen of Seeing: Seeing/Drawing as Meditation*. New York: Vintage Books, 1973.

Gawain, Shakti. *Creative Visualization*. New York: Bantam Books, 1982.

Gibran, Kahlil. *The Prophet*. New York: Alfred A. Knopf, 1971.

Gitlin, Todd (editor). *Watching Television*. New York: Pantheon Books, 1986.

Godman, David (editor). *Be As You Are: The Teachings of Sri Ramana Maharshi*. Boston: Arkana, 1985.

Goldberg, Natalie. *Writing Down the Bones: Freeing the Writer Within*. Boston: Shambhala, 1986.

Gurdjieff, G.I. *Views from the Real World*. New York: E.P. Dutton, 1975.

Hanh, Thich Nhat. *The Miracle of Mindfulness: A Manual on Meditation*. Boston: Beacon Press, 1975.

Hanh, Thich Nhat. *Our Appointment with Life: The Buddha's Teaching on Living in the Present*. Berkeley, CA: Parallax Press, 1990.

Hanh, Thich Nhat. *Peace Is Every Step*. New York: Bantam, 1991.

Hawking, Stephen W. *A Brief History of Time: From the Big Bang to Black Holes*. New York: Bantam Books, 1988.

Hunter, Linda Mason. *The Healthy Home*. Emmaus, PA: Rodale Press, 1989.

Huxley, Aldous. *The Perennial Philosophy*. New York: Harper and Row, 1970.

Iyengar, B. K. S. *The Concise Light on Yoga*. New York: Schocken Books, 1982.

Jampolsky, Gerald. *Love Is Letting Go of Fear*. New York: Bantam, 1981.

Jones, Susan Smith, Ph.D. *Choose to Live Peacefully*. Berkeley, CA: Celestial Arts, 1992.

Kapleau, Roshi Philip. *The Three Pillars of Zen*. Garden City, NY: Anchor Books, 1980.

Key, Wilson Bryan. *Media Sexploitation*. New York: Signet, 1976.

Klipper, Ilse. *Coming Into Harmony*. Palo Alto, CA: Pathways Press, 1992.

Krishnamurti, J. *The First and Last Freedom*. Wheaton, IL: The Theosophical Publishing House, 1954.

Krishnamurti, J. *You Are the World*. New York: Harper & Row, 1972.

Kubey, Robert, Ph.D., and Csikszentmihalyi, Mihaly, Ph.D. *Television and the Quality of Life: How Viewing Shapes Everyday Experience*. Hillside, NJ: Erlbaum Publishers, 1990.

Kübler-Ross, Elisabeth. *On Death and Dying*. New York: Macmillan, 1970.

LaChapelle, Dolores. *Earth Wisdom*. Silverton, CO: Finn Hill Arts, 1978.

Lao-Tzu. *Tao Te Ching*. A new translation by Gia-Fu Feng and Jane English. New York: Vintage Books, 1972.

Larsen, Stephen, Ph.D. *The Mythic Imagination: Your Quest for Meaning through Personal Mythology*. New York: Bantam, 1990.

Lavabre, Marcel. *Aromatherapy Workbook*. Rochester, VT: Healing Arts Press, 1990.

Lawrence, Brother. *Practice of the Presence of God*. Mount Vernon, NY: Peter Pauper Press, 1967.

Leadingham, Carrie; Moschella, Joann E.; and Vartanian, Hilary M. (editors). *Peace Prayers: Meditations, Affirmations, Invocations, Poems, and Prayers for Peace*. San Francisco: Harper Collins, 1992.

Levine, Stephen. *Who Dies?*. New York: Doubleday, 1982.

Lust, John, N.D., D.B.M. *The Herb Book*. New York: Bantam, 1974.

Mehta, Silva, Mira, and Shyam. *Yoga: The Iyengar Way*. New York: Knopf, 1992.

Metzger, Deena. *Writing for Your Life: A Guide and Companion to the Inner Worlds*. San Francisco: Harper, 1992.

Millman, Dan. *No Ordinary Moments: A Peaceful Warrior's Guide to Daily Life*. Tiburon, CA: H J Kramer, 1992.

Mitchell, Stephen (editor). *The Enlightened Heart: An Anthology of Sacred Poetry*. New York: Harper and Row, 1989.

Mitchell, Stephen (editor). *The Enlightened Mind: An Anthology of Sacred Prose*. New York: Harper Collins, 1991.

Moffatt, James, D.D., D.Litt. *The Bible: A New Translation*. New York: Harper, 1950.

New Catholic Edition of the Holy Bible. New York: Catholic Publishing Co., 1957.

Nisker, Wes "Scoop". *Crazy Wisdom*. Berkeley, CA: Ten Speed Press, 1990.

Ouspensky, P.D. *In Search of the Miraculous*. New York: Harcourt Brace Jovanovich, 1977.

Patterson, Meg, MBE, MBChB, FRCSE. *Hooked? NET: The New Approach to Drug Cure*. London: Faber & Faber, Ltd., 1986.

Rajneesh, Bhagwan Shree. *The Book of Secrets*. New York: Harper & Row, 1974.

Rajneesh, Bhagwan Shree. *The Book of Secrets 2*. San Francisco: Harper Colophon Books, 1979.

Rajneesh, Bhagwan Shree. *The Grass Grows by Itself*. Poona, India: Rajneesh Foundation, 1976.

Rajneesh, Bhagwan Shree. *Meditation: The Art of Ecstasy*. New York: Harper Colophon Books, 1976.

Rajneesh, Bhagwan Shree. *Words Like Fire: Discourses on Jesus*. San Francisco: Harper & Row, 1976.

Ram Dass. *Be Here Now*. New York: Crown Publishers, 1971.

Ram Dass. *Journey of Awakening: A Meditator's Guidebook*. New York: Bantam Books, 1978.

Ram Dass and Bush, Mirabai. *Compassion in Action*. New York: Bell Tower, 1992.

Ram Dass and Gorman, Paul. *How Can I Help?* New York: Alfred A. Knopf, 1985.

Ray, Sondra. *Loving Relationships*. Berkeley, CA: Celestial Arts, 1980.

Roberts, Elizabeth and Amidon, Elias (editors). *Earth Prayers from Around the World: 365 Prayers, Poems, and Invocations for Honoring the Earth*. San Francisco: Harper Collins, 1991.

Schriner, Christan, M.S., Rel. D. *Feel Better Now: 30 Ways to Handle Frustration in Three Minutes or Less*. Rolling Hills Estates, CA: Jalmar Press, 1990.

Siegel, Bernie. *Love, Medicine & Miracles*. New York: Harper, 1986.

Smith, Manuel J., Ph.D. *When I Say No I Feel Guilty*. New York: Bantam Press, 1975.

Sun Bear with Mulligan, Crysalis; Nufer, Peter; and Wabun. *Walk in Balance: The Path to Healthy, Happy, Harmonious Living*. New York: Prentice Hall, 1989.

Suzuki, D.T. *An Introduction to Zen Buddhism*. New York: Grove Press, Inc., 1964.

Suzuki, Shunryu. *Zen Mind, Beginner's Mind*. New York: Weatherhill, 1970.

Tierra, Michael, C.A., N.D. *The Way of Herbs*. New York: Washington Square Press, 1980.

Tisserand, Robert B. *The Art of Aromatherapy*. Rochester, VT: Healing Arts Press, 1977.

Voelker, Francis H. and Voelker, Ludmila A. (editors). *Mass Media: Forces in Our Society*, Third Edition. New York: Harcourt Brace Jovanovich, 1978.

Wagner, Jane. *The Search for Signs of Intelligent Life in the Universe*. New York: Harper and Row, 1986.

Watts, Alan. *The Wisdom of Insecurity: A Message for an Age of Anxiety*. New York: Pantheon, 1951.

Welwood, John. *Challenge of the Heart: Love, Sex, and Intimacy in Changing Times*. Boston: Shambhala, 1985.

White Eagle. *The Quiet Mind*. Oxford, England: The White Eagle Publishing Trust, 1972.

Whitman, Walt. *Leaves of Grass*. New York: Vintage Books, 1992.

Williams, Redford, M.D. and Williams, Virginia, Ph.D. *Anger Kills: Seventeen Strategies for Controlling the Hostility That Can Harm Your Health*. New York: Random House, 1993.

Yesudian, Selvarajan and Haich, Elisabeth. *Yoga and Health*. London: Unwin, 1953.

Yogananda, Paramahansa. *Man's Eternal Quest*. Los Angeles: Self-Realization Fellowship, 1975.

Yogananda, Paramahansa. *Scientific Healing Affirmations*. Los Angeles: Self-Realization Fellowship, 1985.

Zukav, Gary. *The Dancing Wu Li Masters: An Overview of the New Physics*. New York: Bantam, 1979.

Index

About the Authors

*O*ver the past fifteen years, **Jerry Dorsman** has evaluated hundreds of techniques that help individuals achieve a calm inner state. He incorporated many of these techniques into his highly successful addiction recovery program.

His first book, *How to Quit Drinking Without A.A.*, was published in March 1991 and quickly became a top-selling recovery book. It sold 23,000 copies during the first two years. A Spanish translation was released for distribution in fall 1993. The book's revised edition was published by Prima Publishing in January 1994.

As an expert on addiction and addiction treatment alternatives, Jerry has appeared on more than 125 radio shows all over the United States and Canada as well as two local TV shows. In addition, articles about his program and book reviews have appeared in *USA Today*, the *Philadelphia Inquirer, Your Health* (cover story), *Natural Health*, and *Better World* magazines, and almost every magazine, newsletter, and newsmagazine in the field of addiction recovery. Jerry has himself written articles on recovery that have appeared in *Professional Counselor, Addiction & Recovery, Journal of Rational Recovery*, the *Northeast Recovery Networker*, and *Journey*.

Jerry is an active member of the National Association of Alcoholism and Drug Abuse Counselors, and his two academic degrees include a high-honors degree in psychology. He currently works for the Division of Mental Health in Cecil County, Maryland, where, aside from administrative responsibilities, he provides group therapy for mental health clients who have problems with drug and alcohol addictions.

Bob Davis, M.A., is a certified yoga teacher and stress management therapist who works with chronically mentally ill adults and sexually abused teenagers. Aside from his clinical work, he has taught yoga and meditation classes in northern Delaware for more than twenty years.

Bob received a Delaware State Arts Council Grant for creative writing in 1989 and won first place in creative writing at the First State Veterans Arts Council in 1987. His work has appeared in *Yoga Journal, The Sun, Phoenix,* and elsewhere. Bob was also editor of the first edition of *How to Quit Drinking Without A.A.* He is currently writing a memoir, *Home on Hillandale,* about his life on the farm where he grew up and still resides.

More Psychology & Self-Help Books
From Prima Publishing

The Tao of Love
by Ivan Hoffman

The time has come for a new way of thinking by seeking out the wisdom of ancient thought. Ivan Hoffman combines the spirituality of Taoism, which dates back 2500 years, with his personal and psychological reflections to make this ancient wisdom all the more relevant today.

Here, Hoffman suggests that in learning to love, people must learn about themselves. Instead of blaming others for their problems, people must learn to untie the noose that chokes off their freedom and their ability to love. When people let go of themselves and their need to be loved, they find love, both from others and from the universe.

The Tao of Money
by Ivan Hoffman

The Tao of Money is not about how to get a better job, or how to invest wisely, or how to earn more money. At least not directly. These may be the results, however, when we come to understand our connection to money and money's connection to economic and political events, and how to adapt that understanding to our own lives. Money is often used as a substitute for self-worth, and how we think about ourselves directly translates into how we spend our money and our time. *The Tao of Money* helps us understand that, by changing the way we think about money, we can change our lives.

Understanding: Eliminating Stress and Finding Serenity in Life and Relationships
by Jane Nelsen

A beautifully quiet guide for self-acceptance, this book will strike a chord among those who are the most demanding and the least forgiving of themselves, especially adult children of alcoholics, parents with troubled relationships with their children, men and women "unlucky" in love, and those with driven personalities.

FILL IN AND MAIL TODAY

PRIMA PUBLISHING
P.O. BOX 1260BK
ROCKLIN, CA 95677

USE YOUR VISA/MC AND ORDER BY PHONE

(916) 632-7400 (M–F 9–4 PST)

Please send me the following titles:

Quantity	Title	Amount
_____	*The Tao of Love* $9.95	_____
_____	*The Tao of Money* $17.95 (hardback)	_____
_____	*Understanding: Eliminating Stress* $9.95	_____
_____	*How to Achieve Peace of Mind* $9.95	_____

Subtotal	$ _____
Postage & Handling ($3.00 for first book plus $1.00 each additional book)	$ _____
7.25 % Sales Tax (California only)	$ _____
TOTAL (U.S. funds only)	$ _____

❏ Check enclosed for $_____ (payable to Prima Publishing)

Charge my   ❏ MasterCard   ❏ Visa

Account No. _____ Exp. Date _____

Signature _____

Your Name _____

Address _____

City/State/Zip _____

Daytime Telephone _____

Satisfaction is guaranteed—or your money back!
Please allow three to four weeks for delivery.
THANK YOU FOR YOUR ORDER